The Un

Kirlian Photog

BRIAN SNELLGROVE

The Unseen Self
Kirlian Photography Explained

Index compiled by
BARBARA NEWBY

SAFFRON WALDEN
THE C.W. DANIEL COMPANY LIMITED

First published in Great Britain in 1979
This completely revised and updated edition
published in 1996 by
The C.W.Daniel Company Limited
1 Church Path, Saffron Walden
Essex, CB10 1JP, England

ISBN 0 85207 277 5

Produced in association with
Book Production Consultants plc
25–27 High Street, Chesterton, Cambridge CB4 1ND
Typeset by Cambridge Photosetting Services
Printed and Bound by Biddles, Guildford

Contents

Illustrations

Foreword

My interest in the whole topic of auras and Kirlian Photography was due to a bunch of daffodils.

My early memories were of post-war austerity, ration books, foggy November afternoons and the feeling of being 'different' as a vicar's son. My triple attendance at church on Sundays as an angelic choirboy provided a natural distance from the congregation. I was separated by my white apparel from the serried rows of hats bobbing up and down in response to the ritual progression of the service. And yet even in my teenage rebellious phase I grew to love the quaint language of the 1662 prayer book. Study and solitary pursuits of reading and gardening took most of my energy.

I passed through the University system largely unaware of who 'I' was. In spite of spending most of my energy organizing the University Charities' Appeal (or 'rag' as it was known in those days) I obtained a BA degree in Social Science. The sight of the rhododendrons clustering along the banks of the oxbow river that surrounded Durham Cathedral often distracted me in my studies.

I had started to become aware in my early twenties of something called the 'New Age'. At a conference in 1973 on Health and Healing I heard talk of reincarnation; life after death; telepathy, and met people who were 'psychic' and some who could apparently see 'auras'. For some reason, this felt like a breath of fresh air.

My traditional family background as a vicar's son in the Church of England hardly fitted with an interest in the esoteric. My teens and most of my 20s had been surrounded by restrictions of the daily routine of survival. It sounded quite daring to even talk about such things as healing or reincarnation. At the Healing conference itself I felt like a child stealing apples from an orchard. Would God in his elevated position of espial notice my departure from the straight and narrow? Surely the participants in this conference could not be 'Christian'? In those times there was a strong link between parapsychology (or para *anything* for that matter) and the works of the devil. It is only now that I realize how ignorant and damaging this dualistic thinking is.

In 1972, at the age of 28, I was introduced to an old Polish priest called Andrew Glazewski. He was in a resident post at a converted army camp in Somerset for displaced Polish ex-servicemen.

The voice on the phone was warm and welcoming and I accepted the invitation instinctively. I remember taking the train from Paddington and wondering what I was letting myself in for. Eastern Europe itself and its people were a closed book to me. I saw this region as a dark and foreboding place and therefore, I reasoned, people from that area would probably be alien to me.

I found the camp and wandered around until I found the right place. There was Andrew at the door, beaming. "Brian, come in" he said, as if he had known me for ages. I relaxed. The ground of my fears dropped away to nothing. I had the great feeling of being understood and accepted. This was an adventure indeed.

Andrew lived in a one-roomed Nissen hut containing an amazing collection of papers, books and correspondence. The kitchen area contained a small stove and a mountain of tins. Next to the cooker stood in all its glory – a lavatory!

I can honestly say that every inch of floor, shelf, wall, alcove, cupboard space had its function. I found a place to sit and we started talking. It was not – to put it mildly – a conventional conversation but full of humour and laughter, of jokes at his own expense. I was bursting with questions that I had not dared to ask anyone else, and something within me gave me the freedom to speak. At the time I was much burdened by my problems of seeing an alien and unfriendly world in a meaningful way. I started to stumble through my list of questions but found that before I had even articulated them, I felt relieved.

Within a few moments of my attempts to communicate, Andrew had taken from his pocket a small pith ball attached to a length of thread. Whilst I was speaking, he held his hand up towards what appeared to be a small anatomical diagram and spun the pith. His hand moved closer to the chart as the 'treatment' progressed. I felt a sense of lightening and relief. It was as if a great burden was being lifted off me. Dare I believe what I saw with my own eyes? I had no option, though my conscious mind fought every inch of the way.

After 20 minutes he stopped. "It's done", he commented. He paused and threw back his head and beamed. "You have healing ability" he said. I remember thinking "I bet he says that to everyone". Deeper down, though, I felt a sense of tumult. Could there be more to me than I had imagined? How could someone cause such blissful feelings just waving a pith ball?

We paused for tea and enjoyed the vivid sunset through the window. In the distance, stooped figures were to be seen going about their daily tasks. How must it feel to be a stranger in exile, when it is so easy to become a stranger in one's own country. Having said that, I have observed that Poles carry their sense of community wherever the are.

The train rattled through the darkening countryside. I stared at the flickering track side as I tried to make sense of the events of the day. I had promised to join my new confidant at a healing course run by the Wrekin Trust that was, by coincidence, being held the following weekend.

Andrew had made me promise to read a book by Harold Saxton Burr entitled *Blueprint for Immortality*. He talked about 'fields' which he classified into two types – thought fields and life fields. The latter are pre-existing electro-magnetic fields into which the body grows; the former being fields which we create by the harmony of our own thoughts. I quickly obtained the book and consumed it in one sitting.

The day of the course dawned. My judgemental mind always groans at the sight of a mixture of rather odd and eccentric people, mostly middle-aged females. However, as we all know, appearances can be deceptive and two or three of them turned out to be fascinating. Andrew himself was going to talk but most of the day was taken up by two ladies from the Radionic Association showing how to 'heal' a patient, who had to lie down on a couch. They stood somewhat dramatically, one at the head, one at the feet and passed their hands over the patient's body. There was no question but that the atmosphere of the room was becoming electric. My hands started to crackle, particularly the left one. I did not attribute significance to it at the time.

At lunch time Andrew suggested we went for a walk. In the grounds of the country house where we were meeting there were enormous elm trees.

At his suggestion, a group of us stood round one tree with our palms uppermost and sent warm thoughts of greeting to it. I felt self-conscious but since there were no outsiders present, it did not seem to matter.

The tree was alive. I pointed my hands towards the centre, and noticed that my palms were hot – as if an electric fire was focused on them. Turning the hands through 90° cancelled out the effect.

The prickles in my hand increased, and I also noticed that these impressions varied according to the distance from the tree. Some of the prickles were in the palm, others along the finger and yet more on the back of the hand.

We finished about 5p.m. and I wandered round the house ending up in the foyer. On impulse, I put up my left hand and looked at the daffodils across the room. I suppose they must have been 20 feet away. I found myself 'willing' them to move. To my surprise and glee, they all started nodding sideways. I 'told' them to stop. They did immediately. Then I said in my mind 'white ones move, yellow ones don't'. Sure enough, the white ones bobbed backwards and forwards for all they were worth. I tried the converse with the same result. As a finale, I got them all to move. Best results were obtained when I looked slightly beyond them. If I stared at them directly no movement was discerned.

A new acquaintance, Gordon Barker, who turned out to be a healer and priest, attended the day, and he happened to be passing. "Gordon," said I, "watch this." I repeated the demonstration. Gordon smiled enigmatically and contented himself with the observation "Mmm, strange". At the time there was no wind, and no doors or windows were open.

Later that evening I went with a friend into the local town, Taunton, for a drink. Behind the bar, lo and behold, were daffodils. Just out of sheet devilment and curiosity I tried the same thing again. The bar maid, obviously not versed in the finer points of healing, described it as 'creepy'. I felt like a child with a new toy.

Next day I returned to London. My newly found gift worked the next morning but it took a much greater effort. The next day, nothing happened in spite of all my concentrations of will power. In a way I was not unduly surprised as I had lost the feeling of being charged, but no there was no question that 'I', or something associated with me, could influence objects at a distance. I did not understand the mechanism, but can best describe it as pushing with the back part of my head. To this day those gently waving daffodils are as clear in my mind as if the event had happened yesterday.

Another component part in my development similarly took me

by surprise. Shortly after the daffodil event I became interested in the pendulum. This was due to simple curiosity after Andrew Glazewski's demonstration with the pith ball. I took an example in my hand for the first time. Nothing happened. It hung from its string like a dead thing. I remember feeling very self-conscious though there was no one to witness the event. I 'cheated' by swinging it. After a few revolutions it stopped. Then my wonderful mind cut in again. 'What a lot of rubbish,' thought I. The cynics were right.

As I thought this, I was conscious of a slight shock in one of my fingers. Although I was now holding the pendulum quite still, it started to gyrate. I felt a 'push' like an invisible hand. I thought 'yes' and it started to swing clockwise; thoughts of 'no' produced an anti-clockwise swing. The shocks in the fingers became more pronounced. I used the pendulum for a variety of purposes for many years to dowse for psychological conditions, blocks, etc. on those present or absent. For much of this time I was too lacking in confidence to use it on anything other than a personal basis. I should add that in 25 years I have had absolutely no success in map dowsing, finding water, and all the others things that dowsers are supposed to do. I thought at one point that the movement was caused by small muscular changes in the hand. I rigged up an apparatus – a sort of clamp – to hold my hand at the fingers and prevent any swing, however minute. When the pendulum was held and I thought of a question, it took much longer to start moving, but movement there was.

Dentists' waiting rooms are tedious places. I try to gear myself to not thinking about the pain and discomfort. I was flicking dreamily through a journal when I spotted a description of an 'aura camera' which was a small object like a lunch box onto which you were apparently supposed to put your hands. An example print showed streamers radiating from a sample hand. I was absolutely transfixed. My eyes shot out on stalks. I HAD to have one. There was no doubt, no question about it. A few telephone calls and within 24 hours the Verograph (so named by the inventor Ted Van Der Veer) was sitting on my living-room table. I rigged up my bedroom at home as a dark-room, bought the necessary basic processing equipment, and started taking pictures.

By no stretch of the imagination were the experiments conducted in a scientific manner. It was the sheer excitement of discovery. I photographed everything that I could think of; hands, feet, foreheads, bread, fruit, potatoes, flowers – even stones. So addictive was this stage that I frequently forgot to eat!

After making a few hundred photos I was still none the wiser about their meaning. Someone asked me to write an article on it and, feeling foolish, I put paper in the typewriter and poised myself to strike the keys, thinking to myself, 'what is this all about?'

Then something unexpected happened that gave me the clue I had been looking for. I received a shock in the fourth finger of my left hand. Of course! What if each finger relates to a certain aspect of our psychologies? What if it related to other disciplines, i.e. the reputed correlation between the lines of the hands and features in the life of the owner? What if it related to the meridians of energy called acupuncture? What if... What if...

Intuitively I labelled each finger thus: thumb – will power; index finger – leadership; middle finger – career (major involvement with life); fourth finger – creativity; fifth finger – spiritual. I assumed the left hand being a part of the left side of the body would correlate with the right brain (conceptual, feeling, intuition) and similarly the right hand with the left brain (logical, sequential, process-orientated). For some reason, left or right handedness does not seem to make a difference to the readings.

These were the heady days of the New Age, of post flower-power meditation, and as an expression of this the Festivals of Mind, Body and Spirit were launched at Olympia, London. I was invited to take space and with great trepidation I wrote a cheque for £293 for a small 4m × 3m stall. This was intended for experimentation only and I doubted if I would get more than half a dozen people per hour. I thought I would just cover my costs. Ten minutes after the opening on the first day, the queue was 10 deep. I did not stop for the whole exhibition. Without realizing it, I had tapped into something more than curiosity. There is a desire to SEE energies that had hitherto been invisible; a need to be able to believe in life forces beyond the physical. During this first year at the Festival and in succeeding years, I must have had sight of over 10,000 examples of hands. I can say without exaggeration that no two prints are the same.

The Kirlian energetic field information can be used in several ways as explained in this book. Overall it provides a unique fingerprint; an appreciation of strong and weak points; a determination of the balance between mind (thinking), body (functioning), spirit (dynamism).

It can be used to see which areas need assistance and strengthening. It is ideally suited for corroboration with other disciplines such as acupuncture, homoeopathy and therapy because the image responds instantly to changes in the field.

Is this 'diagnosis'? There are many Kirlian practitioners and researchers, possibly 100 machines in use in the UK, and several thousand machines in operation worldwide. Some are using it as a back-up diagnostic tool to give another perspective on their own discipline (homoeopathy, acupuncture etc). Many are cautious about the use of such a visually powerful method in connection with the term 'diagnosis' and prefer to use it as part of an overall appreciation of the dynamics and harmonies of the subject.

In the longer term, Kirlian photography is becoming part of a much wider trend towards an understanding of the nature of man viewed as a whole. For decades now, medicine based on technological developments has produced great advances in treatment of disease symptoms, but we have also seen an increase in those who are suffering from the nature of the treatment methods, whether by drugs or chemotherapy or indeed invasive surgery.

The public is becoming increasingly interested in holistic methods of understanding the human condition, where psychological conditions are considered along with the immediate physical presenting symptom. Treatments such as 'spiritual healing' are felt by many to be more appropriate for some types of conditions.

I anticipate the scepticism of many who are of a scientific disposition. When I started this work I was completely open-minded. When others started their own Kirlian work they were completely sceptical and were, I believe, won over by the sheer weight of evidence. It is up to you, the reader, to decide if the observed changes could be explained by changes in physical parameters such as pressure and temperature.

This book will be giving an overview of some of the work that has been done. It explains the methodology in some detail and discusses possible ways in which the energies that surround an object or person can be understood.

Historically speaking, I believe there was a time when man did not need machines to 'see'. Reliance on machines may indicate that we with a twentieth century mentality may be the primitives, rather than those to whom we rather patronizingly refer as primitive peoples.

This book is written in the hope that more scientists and medically qualified people, and anyone interested in deepening their understanding of the human condition will see the possibilities of this method as a 'peep into the cathedral', and as a means of helping mankind discover more of the hidden potential within.

Brian Snellgrove, Dulwich, 1995
c/o 102 Thurlow Park Road, London SE21 8HY
Email briansnellgrove@POBox.com

*The Scientific and Medical Network, a charity registered in the UK aims to deepen understanding in science, medicine and education by fostering both rational and intuitive insights. Founded in 1973, it has over 1,350 members in 52 countries and specializes in questioning the assumptions of contemporary scientific and medical thinking, 'so often limited by exclusively materialistic and reductionistic thinking'.

*Lesser Halings, Tilehouse Lane, Denham, Middx, UB9 5DG. Phone/fax – (00 44) 01895 835818

~ I ~

Historical aspects of the human energy field

To Miss Zheng Xianling, the existence of the human energy field is an everyday fact. In 1988, she worked at the People's Liberation Army general staff headquarters in Peking. She possessed a very unusual type of clairvoyance; three-dimensional X-ray vision – in colour. She diagnosed her fully-clothed patients in the dark and claimed to see their bones, veins and internal organs glowing before her eyes. So impressive was her work that her waiting list was two years long.

Before examining the history of Kirlian photography itself, let us have a look at attitudes towards the human energy field – as it is now called – over the centuries.

Every school pupil has seen the effect on iron filings on a piece of paper when a magnet is placed underneath, and also how the energy fields of two magnets can interfere with each other when they get close enough – but what of an effect round living things?

The human energy field can be defined as an emanation from a person not visible to the naked eye under normal circumstances and chiefly encircling the head. It is described as a cloud of light encircling the person or – in mystical terms – an envelope of the body, mind, and spirit. It appears to consist of subtle elements – the blue seen by some clairvoyants and the light effect seen around the heads of saints, and more gross elements including a great variety of electric fields, only some of which we are currently able to measure.

Very few people, even practising clairvoyants, can see the colours of the aura consistently. The level, volatility or disposition of the aura reflects partly in colour though the regularity is just as important. According to the clairvoyants, the colours can change from moment to moment and usually vary with mood swings. Be those facts as they may, there is no independent corroboration from scientists or indeed a method of measuring the wavelength differentials, coming as they appear to do from the body in three-dimensions. Also if we see an aura through our own energy field, it is likely to be distorted by our own pre-dispositions. If I look at a landscape through a red filter, all colours will have their red element taken out of them. Sublimity, spiritual elevation and objectivity is required for accurate observation. For similar reasons, therapists and psychiatrists undergo a period of personal analysis themselves before becoming qualified.

From sight of the colours, clairvoyants draw inferences as to the emotional and spiritual state of the subject, including disease and imbalance. The use of the word clairvoyant was originally a pragmatic word derived from the French 'seeing clearly', a combination of two words 'clair' + 'voyant'. In this modern reductionist world the word is sometimes used in a pejorative and often dismissive way, describing a person who makes somewhat suspect claims to a gullible audience about their own abilities.

There is no standard scale of colours but there is general agreement amongst more clairvoyants about the meaning of colours, which are by no means limited to the pure colours of the spectrum. Annie Bessant and C. W. Leadbeater in their book *Thought Forms* describe not only the predominant colour in the aura to which they ascribe meaning, but a variety of shapes associated with 'sudden fright', 'greed for drink', 'at a street accident', etc. They say that the body under the impulse of thought 'throws off a vibrating portion of itself, shaped by the nature of the vibrations... and this gathers from the surrounding atmosphere matter similar to itself in fineness from the elemental essence of the mental world'.

For the beginner, however, the following will suffice. These are the colours associated with predominant states of mind.

White (very rare!) – a very highly spiritually evolved being;

Violet – very psychic, spiritual, the psychic faculty, spirituality, regality, spiritual power arising from knowledge and occult pre-eminence;

Blue – creative and spiritual. Clear creative channels. Religious feeling and devotion;

Green – good affinity between body and soul, a colour of varied significance; its root meaning is the placing of oneself in the position of another person. In its lower aspects it represents deceit and jealousy; higher up in the emotional scale it signifies adaptability; and at its very highest when it represents the colour of foliage, sympathy – the very essence of feeling for other people. In some shades, green stands for the lower intellectual and critical faculties, merging into yellow;

Yellow – personal power and highly developed intellect;

Orange – intellect used for selfish ends, pride and ambition;

Red – vitality and health on the physical plane: anger. Rose red to mean pure affection; brilliant red – anger and force; dirty red – passion and sensuality; brown – avarice.

The accumulation of observations is that each individual emits his or her own characteristic pattern. Auras are mainly linked with the human being; plants and stones also radiate after a fashion, but because they cannot think in the way we understand it, their fields are more pre-determined by their physical and physiological state and are less likely to vary.

The modern term for any sensation of light for which there is no apparent physical cause is photism. Many examples are cited in the Bible, including the dazzling light encountered by Moses at the burning bush, and on Mount Sinai when he descended with the tablets engraved with the Ten Commandments. The light shining around him was so bright that the children of Israel were unable to look upon it. An exceedingly brilliant light shone around St. Paul when he had his vision at the time of his conversion on the road to Damascus. It is reputed that when St. John of the Cross knelt at prayer at the altar, a 'certain brightness' darted from his face. St. Philip Neri was constantly seen enveloped in light.

This light was known in Hebrew as the Shekinah, or luminous Presence of God. The Shekinah appears in art as the aureole (or aureola, diminutive of the Latin **aura**).

Medieval saints and mystics distinguished four different types of aura; the Nimbus, the Halo, the Aureola and the Glory. The first two are reputed to stream from the head (possibly an indication of the health of the crown 'chakra'), the aureola from the whole body and the Glory is a combination of the two. The word 'chakra' is Sanskrit for wheel or circle, and these vortices have a circular, whirling appearance as they draw various forces and energies into the body. In the words of C. G. Jung, they are the gateways of consciousness in man, receptive points for the inflow of energies from the cosmos and the spirit and soul of men.

Incidentally, the word 'Aura' as the energy field is referred to by some, comes from the Latin **air**, which in turn comes from the Greek word for breeze, or breath. The word 'aura' is not only a term for a unique vibrational field we radiate as individuals, but an expression of a collective vibrational field which is generated by society and indeed mankind as a whole. This sum of all endeavours, its harmony or disharmony, probably has a significant effect on the events of our planet. Indeed the planet itself has an aura – primarily the earth's magnetic field – as a backdrop to which is added the cocktail of electromagnetic field effects from radio and TV stations, high voltage lines, etc. This impinges on us all both individually and collectively.

The existence of a human energy field has been reported for many thousands of years in all parts of the globe. In many of the sacred books of the East, representations of the great teachers and holy men are given with the light extending round the whole of the body. Instances of this may be found in the temple caves of India and Sri Lanka, in the Japanese Buddhistic books, also in Egypt, Greece, Mexico and Peru.

Ancient Indian spiritual tradition – over 5,000 years old – referred to a universal energy called 'Prana'. This universal energy is seen as the basic constituent and source of all life.

The Chinese, in the third millenia BC, posited the existence of vital energy, which they called 'Chi'i'. All matter, animate and inanimate, is composed of, and pervaded with this universal energy. This 'Chi'i' contains two polar forces, the yin and the yang. When the yin and the yang are balanced in an organism, the living systems exhibit physical health; when they are unbalanced a diseased state results. Over-powerful yang results in excessive organic activity; predominant yin makes for insufficient functioning, both resulting in physical illness. The ancient art of acupuncture treatment focuses on balancing the yin and the yang.

The dual flows of energy are expressed in everything in the universe, day and night, hot and cold, life and death, etc. Crudely speaking yin is the female polarity; yang the male polarity. Everything has its force of opposition but this opposition, by its very existence, is itself complementary. Yang tends to stimulate and is the positive principle, while yin tends to sedate, and is the negative principle. Health is dependent on the equilibrium of yin and yang, firstly within the body and secondarily within the entire universe.

This vital body perceived as a luminous body was first recorded in western literature by the Pythagoreans in about 500 BC. They held that its light could produce a variety of effects in the human organism including the cure of illness.

Pythagoras himself used musical vibrations, colour and poetry to cure disease. Cabala, the Jewish mystical theosophy which arose in the seventh century AD refers to these same energies as the 'astral light'. Christian religious paintings portray spiritual figures surrounded by a field of light.

The idea of an energy pervading all nature has been held by many minds of the highest intellect. The alchemist Theophrastus Bombastus von Hohenheim, better known as Paracelsus, described the aura in the sixteenth century as follows:

"The vital force is not enclosed in man, but radiates round him like a luminous sphere, and it may be made to act at a distance. In these semi-natural rays the imagination of man may produce healthy or morbid effects. It may poison the essence of life and cause diseases, or it may purify it after it has been made impure, and restore the health."

He also said:

"Our thoughts are simply magnetic emanations, which in escaping from our brains, penetrate into kindred heads and carry hither, with a reflection of our life, the mirage of our secrets."

This period of history saw the division between the alchemists and the clinicians. The former complained that modern medicine had left the ways of nature and created artificial systems of treatment. Paracelsus christened the knife-wielding clinicians of the time 'butchers'. He himself found many natural cures for a variety of diseases using charms, herbs, music and colours. It appears he could see the aura, for he described white colours in the vital envelope relating to health and goodness, whilst those tinged with black represented disharmony and evil. In general he was considered the greatest healer of his time.

Helmont, a philosopher, visualized a universal fluid which pervades all nature, and is not a corporal or a condensable matter but a pure vital spirit that penetrates all bodies.

Leibnitz wrote that the essential elements of the universe are centres of force containing their own well-spring of motion.

The first scientific studies to show that light is emitted by biological samples was probably done in the late 1600s by Boyle who observed that the light emitted by bacteria was dependent on the presence of oxygen.

Electrically produced images have a long history for in 1777 in Germany, George Christian Lichtenberg first described the images produced by an electrostatic discharge, and he saw this process as a way of studying the 'electric fluid'. In 1778 he presented a paper to the Royal Society of Science where he observed 'the phenomenon is able to exert light in itself from the hand'.

In the late 1800s the French physiologist, DuBois, studied the phenomenon of bioluminescence in primitive organisms and postulated that the light emissions were due to the chemical oxidation of a non-specific group of substances which he called luciferins.

Although it had been acknowledged beyond dispute that the human body is a chemical machine, evidence started to accumulate with more and more insistence that the functionings of the body were not only chemical in nature, but also included significant magnetic, electrical and energetic elements. These ideas go back at least to the time of Mesmer in the 1800s. He reported that animate and inanimate objects could be charged with a fluid, and that in general, 'living matter has a property susceptible to being acted on by earthly and celestial magnetic forces'. Mesmer postulated that the entire universe is filled with a fluid less perceptible than gas in which all matter is immersed, and that the fluid carries vibrations in its substance. He suggested that the vibrations of this fluid, permeating as it did the entire universe, caused all existing physical phenomena. Mesmer, who was a physician and a natural scientist, also believed that each living body causes a direct influence upon other living bodies transmitted through a vibration of the ether.

Mesmer confirmed an earlier discovery that magnets had healing power, and it was in the course of such studies that he found that his hands emitted an energy that he named 'animal magnetism', because he found that its therapeutic effects were similar to that of physical magnetism of permanent magnets he had previously worked with, and which eventually caused him to abandon healing experiments with magnets.

Though his ideas were considered wrong by the majority of the medical and scientific population of the time, his ideas aroused great interest throughout Europe and America. One of those to take an interest was scientist John Elliotson, who was one of the founders of University College Hospital in London. The opposition to Mesmer's ideas in official circles was so strong that it confronted in subsequent decades and centuries any physician or scientist who tried to introduce similar ideas into the community, even ideas that merely tried to show that there was an electro-magnetic energy associated with the body.

Only recently, with the development of the extremely sensitive SQUID magnetometer, has hard core evidence been forthcoming that there is an electromagnetic radiation that is constantly being emitted from other parts of the body, and that when some people bring their hands close to the bodies of others, there is a change in the frequency and amplitude of the waves which are being emitted by the hands. Mesmer discerned such as emission from the hands long ago, and was the forerunner of the scientific discoveries today when he christened this radiation 'animal magnetism'.

Dr. John T. Zummerman has shown that the hands may also emit an electromagnetic radiation whose frequency and amplitude change when some people, notably healers, bring their hands close to the body of the subject. Therefore, the idea that the body may be a bioenergetic or electromagnetic machine as well as a chemical one, has evidence in its favour.

To return to our historical treatise: Boirac and Liebeault (early eighteenth century) saw that humans have a similar energy that can cause an interaction between individuals at a distance. They reported that one person can affect another's health just by their presence.

During the 1800s the famous German chemist and industrialist Baron von Reichenbach (1788–1869) made a substantial contribution by his discovery of paraffin and creosote. He travelled extensively over France, Austria and Germany examining the construction and commercial utilization of ironworks. However, what consumed his energy more and more was his interest in the mysteries of electricity and magnetism which occupied 30 years of this creative life. He became aware of a life-force associated with living people which he dubbed 'odic force' or 'od' for short, named after the Norse god Odin, to suggest the idea of a force with a power that cannot be obstructed that quickly penetrates and courses through everything in the universe.

In order to make observations of the odic force, von Reichenbach used the services of many sensitives and clairvoyants. Many of the 200 people in this category had scientific backgrounds; at least 50 were physicians, chemists, mathematicians or philosophers. We can assume that their reports contained a high degree of accuracy and objectivity.

He found that the observed od from magnets and human subjects exhibited many properties which were similar. He determined that the poles of a magnet not only exhibit the normal magnetic polarity but also a unique polarity associated with this 'odic field'. Magnets gave off a particularly bright light at the poles, the north being surrounded by a white light merging into the layers of red, yellow, green and finally blue. The middle of the magnet gave off a glowing green haze, and the south pole an even brighter white than the north, merging into red. If lengths of wire were exposed outdoors to sunshine, the odic energy rang along the wire into the laboratories and appeared as flame-like emanations from the other end. This energy was also observed to surround the human body, and in particular seen to flow from the fingertips.

In addition to visual sightings, they reported that such fields felt "hot, and red or unpleasant" or "blue and cold and pleasant" to the touch.

His observers found that other objects such as crystals exhibit this unique polarity property without themselves being magnetic.

He found that the force vectors in the human body produced features similar to those present in magnets – and indeed crystals – along their major axes. Based on his experimental evidence he described the left side of the body as a negative pole and the right side as a positive pole. This is a concept similar to the ancient Chinese yin and yang principles mentioned above. Many of his conclusions and accounts are identical with the results of the Russian experiments with colour photography (see below). His sensitives observed in the human aura "flares of green, red and orange and violet, appearing and disappearing. Violet red appearing and dying away in a smoke-like vapour, all intermingled with many small, brilliant sparkles or stars". (2.3)

Meanwhile, in the USA, Dr. Edwin Babbitt (1829–1905) was involved in his own investigations of the life-force. Babbitt enjoyed the advantage of being clairvoyant and could make his observations first hand. He used colour in his healing work and even today his book *The Principles of Light and Colour* is a classic. His view of the human aura is poetic indeed, and he referred to "fountains of light pouring towards me from luminous centres merging into all the iridescent splendours on their way. Sometimes, radiations would flow out from me and become lost to view in the distance … what was more marvellous than almost anything else was the infinite millions of radiations, emanations and luminous currents which at times I would see streaming from and into and through all things, and filling all the surrounding space with coruscations and lightning activities."

Dr. Babbitt claimed that psycho-magnetic curving lines of force surround the human body, and the human head in particular. These lines of force can be mentally projected towards other people in order to tap their aura and make them turn around.

The advent of Nikola Tesla's inventions (see next chapter) sparked many important discoveries in the field of biological energy. One of these was made by William Roentgen, a medical researcher, at St. Thomas's Hospital in London, who pioneered scientific research on 'rays of an unknown origin' which he dubbed 'X-rays'. He found them to have among the shortest frequencies in the electromagnetic spectrum. As we all know, the X-ray has become a commonplace diagnostic tool in medicine.

A colleague of his was Walter Kilner, a medical electrician and member of London's Royal College of Surgeons, convinced of the reality of the human aura. In his book *The Human Aura* – based on four years' work – he wrote: "There cannot be the least doubt of the reality of the existence of an aura enveloping a human being, and this in a short time will be a universally accepted fact."

He speculated that 'magnetic radiations' might be more perceptible to sensitives because the radiation appeared to belong to the ultraviolet frequency, outside the range of sight under normal circumstances.

It is likely that our naked eye is more geared to detecting ultra-violet light than we realize. Detection mechanisms in our eyes comprise rods (around 18 million of them) and cones (about 3 million). They are geared to pick up different wavelengths of light. Cones see visible light. Rods do not recognise colours – everything looks greyish blue. The rods are not affected by red light or light with longer wavelengths, but are stimulated by ultraviolet light.

The auric surround – as seen by sensitives – is never visible in strong light nor in broad daylight. Kilner was well aware of Reichenbach's work with the odic force and with sensitives, but Kilner wanted to see the aura for himself, and he sought a method less dependent on psychic abilities which would be more useful to others. He wrote:

> *"From the first moment of perceiving the human atmosphere, I determined to investigate the subject apart from all occultism; and to remain unbiased, did not read any accounts of the aura until a large number of my patients had been inspected."*

To bring the emanations of the human aura within the range of normal vision, he constructed coloured screens consisting of two hermetically sealed pieces of glass containing an alcohol solution of dicyanine, a coal-tar dye. He enclosed such a dicyanine screen with the first edition of his book *The Human Atmosphere* published in 1911. By training with these screens, Kilner believed that anyone could see at least some of the human energy field. Readers of the book were advised to look through the screen in daylight then turn the eye to view a naked person in dim light before a dark background. Readers would see three distinct types of radiations.

Kilner theorized this was possible because the screens affected the night-seeing nerves of the retina – called retinal rods – enabling the subject to see shorter wavelengths than would normally be possible. Kilner regarded the human energy field as an objective emanation and believed that under the right conditions 95% of the population could see an aura. This is clearly over-optimistic since many people are unable to perceive auras even under suitable conditions. Other factors include the complexity and focus of the mind at the time.

Kilner himself described the aura as a faint, colourful mist surrounding the body and extending from it in all directions. This mist had three zones; a quarter inch layer closest to the skin surrounded by a two inch layer streaked perpendicularly to the body and, lastly, somewhat further out, a delicate exterior luminosity with indefinite contours about six inches across. Kilner found that the appearance of the 'aura' differs considerably from subject to subject depending on age, sex, mental ability and health. Certain diseases showed as patches or irregularities in the human energy field that led Kilner to develop a system of diagnosis of the colour, texture, volume and general appearance of this 'envelope'. Kilner may have been especially clairvoyant and it is not known if his pupils could see the colours as he could.

Some of his subjects could voluntarily change the nature and extent of their aura through mental concentration. Women of an excitable nature showed the greatest facility for this gift. Like Reichenbach, Kilner experimented with magnets and found that if he held a magnet near the body, the aura became more brilliant in that area, and as the force grew the brilliance gathered into a single ray of light. If the magnet was moved, the ray moved with it. Kilner noted that the mutual attraction of two human auras was far greater than that between an aura and a magnet. Exposure to static electricity from a Wimshurst machine caused a speedy and partial collapse of the outer aura, whilst the inner aura lost its distinctness. Continued charging of the aura with static electricity caused the entire auric field to vanish.

Further observations on the medical side revealed that the aura of pathological cases changed in shape and size in response to stimuli, and in cases of nervous diseases such as epilepsy and hysteria it stayed distorted. Impairment of mental facilities caused a lessening in size and distinctness of the aura. People with limited intelligence had auras that were coarse-grained, grey and dull. These sorts of experiments led Kilner to believe that the aura had an intimate connection with the central nervous system.

Following on his work, Oscar Bagnall, a Cambridge biologist, set out to duplicate his work and published a book *The Origins and Properties of the Human Aura* in 1937. Bagnall used for his screens a cheaper substitute in the form of a more stable coal-tar dye. Bagnall's findings were similar to Kilner's in that he saw an inner aura emanating about eight centimetres from the body and an outer aura or haze extending up to a further twenty centimetres. He felt that a proportion of Kilner's sightings was due to his gift of clairvoyance, which was probably greater than Kilner realized. Bagnall postulated that all living things have an aura, which ceases on death. He was among the first to suggest that auric light was perceived with the rods in the receptor field of the eye and was seen by peripheral not focused vision.

A sensitive person claims to see four distinct elements in the aura. C. W. Leadbeater considers the human aura to be roughly egg-shaped. There are four principle types of aura, which relate to various levels of the human consciousness:

The etheric or vital body, which controls and unifies the cosmic or life energy as it relates to the physical body and health;

The astral or emotional body which registers the individual's feelings, desires or sensory facilities;

The mental body which reacts to thoughts generated or received;

The casual body which registers the potential of the individual for their future development.

Currently there is no scientific method of recording these bodies as discrete entities, though Kirlian photography, and some of the other techniques mentioned here, may indeed record an aspect of them.

I am frequently asked if I can 'see' the aura, as if this is some sort of ultimate test for spiritual development. I cannot see, nor ever have been able to see, the aura.

In practice the value of seeing colours as a guide for diagnosis is questionable. For a method to be objective and therefore communicable through teaching it would be necessary to produce a body of people who could see similar colours from the same person exhibiting the same disease.

The part of the electromagnetic spectrum devoted to colour is very small and the radiations of other wavelengths are arguably more significant. Also, this brings in a general question of perception. We may think we are seeing something without normal vision but the information may be being fed to our minds via other routes. An

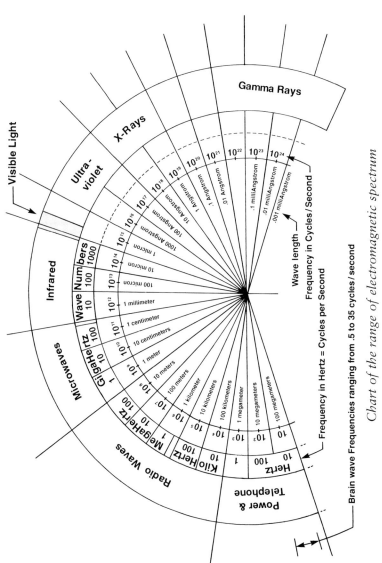

Chart of the range of electromagnetic spectrum

example is that one person may see a detailed and tangible apparition in a room; the person next to them may see nothing. Is there any point in paying attention to colour, always assuming one can see it in the first place? Provided one notices the regularity as well as the colour itself, it provides an indication of the sort of behaviour to be expected. For example a person with a red aura is regarded as more likely to exhibit anger and territoriality. It does not mean that they will always display a given set of characteristics. The question of colour and subjectivity must be a continuing topic of investigation.

It should be borne in mind that as a proportion of the electromagnetic spectrum, visible light only constitutes a very small part. All 'black bodies' emit radiation depending on their temperature. Human beings emit a certain type of radiation above and beyond that expected from its black body properties. These emissions are integrally linked to biological processes. The electromagnetic spectrum is composed of different types of energies which differ in their energy content and frequency.

Low frequency radiation such as radio waves have a lower energy than higher frequency microwaves. Light is at a higher level, and the visible light region is a very small part of the electromagnetic spectrum between infrared and ultraviolet.

The human body also emits other types of radiation including thermal energy, mechanical energy, gamma radiation and acoustic energy.

Acoustic waves are generated by vibration of large molecules, cells and even whole organs. This is in contrast to electromagnetic radiation which is generated by vibrating atoms and subatomic particles. Acoustic radiation is composed of waves of different frequencies and can store and transfer energy. Waves with a frequency below 20 KHz (cycles per second) are called infrasound and those above 20 KHz are known as ultrasound. Although these acoustic waves are inaudible, they have been measured emanating from certain species including man and are believed to be involved in communication. The human aura is therefore likely to consist of a complex interaction between all the above types of radiation. Complex coherent patterns thereby generated may have unknown properties which cannot be readily explained in scientific terminology. The problem is that many scientific methodologies only allow measurements of the individual components of the aura and not their interactions.

Meanwhile, there is much recent discussion and hard scientific evidence about the existence of fields surrounding living things. A modern-day martyr and revolutionary thinker, Rupert Sheldrake, has been propounding the idea of morphic resonance (an energy surrounding all living things) but this has been pre-dated by several people including English researcher George de la Warr in the 1930s. He developed radionics, a system of detection, diagnosis and healing from a distance, utilizing the human biological energy field. Using a portable multi-oscillator as a detector, he discovered and measured accurately standing waves or, as he called them, 'Nodal Points' around the human body which had a markedly higher potential than the surrounding air.

The arrangement of these points was three-dimensional, and appeared to be influenced by changes in the emotions of the subject as well as the influence of other people coming into proximity with the subject. Not only are the energies three dimensional, but varied around, and within, a human body or other living thing.

This discovery was made around the time that Harold Saxton Burr did his work at various institutions in the United States, including Yale University.

In the 1930s, G. Grile, in his book *The Phenomena of Life* with G. Lakhowsky and his publication *L'oscillation Cellulaire* postulated the theory that every cell is an electromagnetic resonator, able to emit and absorb radiations of very high frequency. The theories propound that life is a dynamic evolution of all cells, the harmony – or otherwise – of multiple radiations, which react upon one another. The living cell is like a radio apparatus, able both to transmit and receive waves. The limitations of our senses prevent us from perceiving the radiations from living things; this limited sensory capacity also excludes from the field of direct awareness almost all the electromagnetic spectrum.

Grile also pointed out that electrical energy plays a fundamental part in the organization, growth and function of protoplasm. He wrote:

> "*It is clear that radiation produces the electric current which operates the mechanism as a whole, producing memory, reason, imagination, emotion, secretions, muscular action, the response to infection, normal growth, and the growth of benign tumours and cancers. All these are governed by the*

*electric charges which are generated by the short-wave or ion-
izing radiation in protoplasm."*

The basis of Lakhowsky's theory rests on the principle that life is created by radiation and maintained by it. Grile stated that man is a
radio-electrical mechanism and stressed the significant fact that when
life ends, radiation ends. In fact, the entire system of living beings is
controlled by radiant and electrical forces in the environment. It is
moreover evident that the 'spectrum of living matter' reflects innu-
merable environmental changes and is itself changing continually in
consciousness, in sleep, in emotion, and in every adaptive reaction.

By way of further commentary on radiations, the French scientist
Albert Nodon showed in 1927 that beetles, flies, spiders and other
living insects emit considerable radiations, producing ionization similar to the action of radioactivity. He could find no radiations from
dead matter. Nodon concluded that the vital cells from human organisms, in particular the human body, emit electrons generated by an
actual radiation whose intensity would seem to be much more considerable than that observed in insects and plants. Further "the electrons that are produced in tissues are as a result of electric polariza-
tion due to the absorption of certain radiation quanta coming from
outside the organism".

Nodon was able to obtain "spontaneous radio-photographs" by
placing living things such as plants, insects, etc. directly onto photographic plates. We have to determine what aspects of light energy are
as a result of internal generation, or the impingement of external
energies – for example the sun's energy – and the selective reaction of
the cellular structures to its energy.

It was his view that the whole universe was knit together by a
"universal plexus of cosmic rays" and all forms of matter, ranging
from rarefied gases to solid rock are simply varying degrees of con-
densation in this plexus. Within the world of radiation, everything
lives, moves and has its being.

According to Soviet scientists, electromagnetic cellular emissions
extend from the radio band up to ultraviolet light. The first evidence
that such cellular radiations exist can be traced back to the 1920s
when the Soviet histologist, Alexander Gurwitch, noted in cell
growth experiments that cells seemed to emit some kind of ray, which
he termed 'mitogenic' or 'mitotic' since it seemed related to cell repro-

duction by division, or mitosis. Although Gurwitch had biological evidence that such a ray existed, he did not succeed in capturing it on film in his day. In fact, it was not until the early 1960s that workers at Leningrad State University succeeded in capturing the mitotic rays on sensitive photomultiplier devices. The radiation appears to be in the ultraviolet waveband between 190 and 350 nanometres. This radiation does not resemble other kinds of phosphorescence or luminescence known to biology. As well as this mitogenetic radiation, there are emissions from the cell and cell organelles at other frequencies, including the visible part of the spectrum. The mitogenetic radiation today is called in Soviet textbooks 'dark chemoluminescence in the UV'.

In 1932 Erich Muller, a Swiss geophysicist and engineer, discovered that "energy emanating from man under certain circumstances and certain conditions of health can be conducted along a wire, affecting photographic plates".

In the 1930s, embryologist Dr. Harold Saxton Burr of Yale University and his colleague Dr. F. Northrup devoted themselves to the examination of electromagnetic fields around living objects, and in 1935 published their work under the title *The Electro-Dynamic Theory of Life*. They perfected an ultra-sensitive vacuum tube voltmeter which could measure voltages as small as one millionth of a volt between two points within or on a living system.

Early experiments showed electrical variations in the infrastructure of a tree. An electrode placed on the cambium layer of a tree showed a difference in potential between it and another electrode fixed vertically over the other at a distance of two or three feet. In a 30 year period of monitoring trees, Burr found that they displayed a daily L-field rhythm, peaking at midday with a minimum at night.

In another set of experiments with human female subjects, Dr. Burr measured the voltage differences between the cervix and a distant part of the body – usually the ankle. He found that there was an increased voltage lasting about 24 hours, which occurred in the middle of the menstrual cycle.

Burr called these energy fields of living organisms L-fields (life fields). These fields are like a jelly mould which surround and interpenetrate all living organisms and ensure constant regeneration of our body according to the pattern of our uniqueness (otherwise our friends would not recognise us!).

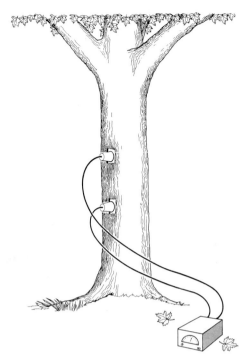

Measurement being taken of voltage variations in a tree

However, another type of field appeared to have continuous, mostly cyclical variations. Some of these variations coincided with the diurnal cycle (or the so-called circadian rhythms, that is the twenty-four hour cycle), others coincide with the sunspot cycle, which – as has clearly been demonstrated by other researchers – is related to planetary configurations. Yet others coincided with the lunar cycle, and so on.

Burr uses this electrical method to predict illness through the changes in direct current potential before any physical symptoms of illnesses could be detected. These pioneering studies have been confirmed, at least in part, by Professor Becke who has also shown that D.C. potentials are involved with several types of healing and regeneration processes occuring naturally in the body. He also showed a correlation between these potentials and the traditional acupuncture system. Alternating current potentials are also found on the surface of the body and have been used extensively in conventional science – measured with an electroencephalogram (EEG) or an electrocardiogram (ECG) and are well known to be correlated with abnormal

functioning of the brain and heart, or indeed the muscles (elec-
tromyograms). The psycho-galvanic reflect meter – known as the lie
detector – indicates the subjects' emotional reactions by measuring
variations in the electrical activity of the brain when responding to
questions.

The scientific community dismissed Burr's work as ridiculous,
and did so without bothering to check his scientific data. Had they
done so they would have read about and discovered for themselves
the electrical fields that he wrote about and could have offered their
own alternative hypothesis. Like the Catholic church bishops who
refused to look through Galileo's telescope, they declined.

A star pupil of Burr's was Dr. Leonard Ravitz who demonstrated
in 1948 that subjects under hypnosis showed marked changes in their
voltage gradients. He found that mentally unstable people displayed
varied and erratic patterns in the voltage potential of their L-fields,
and that it would be possible to predict accurately the forthcoming
reactions of seriously disturbed mental patients.

To repeat, then, Burr discovered that the L-field exists by itself
before any trace can be seen of the physical formation to which it corresponds. Therefore, it cannot be an emanation from the physical
structure itself. Burr concluded that the L-field is the organizing principle behind physical structures, or in other words a programme that
organizes the atoms and molecules into cells and organs, condition-
ing them to perform certain functions.

Although this idea was only investigated scientifically for the first
time in the 1930s, the same conclusion was reached in the early years
of this century by the vitalistic theory – developed by the embryologist Hans Dreisch – that life cannot be explained by normal physical
laws and requires some sort of extra ingredient which he christened
'life force' or 'elan vital' which infuses biological systems and
accounts for their extraordinary powers and abilities. Dreisch postulated the existence of a causal factor operating in living matter called
entelechy after the Greek *telos*, from which the word *teleology*
derives. The implication is that the perfect and complete idea of the
living organism exists in advance and that they contain within themselves a blueprint or plan of action to produce the finished individual.
Dreisch's ideas have fallen out of use, partly because he could not
explain how entelechy could temporarily suspend microbiological
processes, and affect timing and movement of molecular structures.

This is perhaps unfortunate, since in nature it is necessary to produce an explanation for the ability of many animals to reconstitute themselves. For example, if flatworms are chopped up they develop into several complete worms. Salamanders can regenerate an entire new limb if one is removed. If a hydra, a simple creature consisting of a trunk crowned by tentacles, is minced into pieces and left, it will reassemble itself in its entirety.

Some work conducted in Russia in the late 1980s backs up the work of Burr and Langston Day. Two Russian scientists – the engineer and inventor Yuri Kravchenko and the physician Nikolai Kalashchenko – have developed an original instrument; the phase aurometer. This is a highly sensitive instrument for the remote measurement of the electromagnetic radiation of any object up to one and a half metres from the surface. A medical version of the aurometer is in use at the Republican Clinical Hospital in Ufa (Bashkortostan) and it is used to record patients' radiations for diagnostic purposes.

The apparatus is designed to analyse the human electromagnetic field in the 0.5–15.0 KHz range. By the use of electronic filters to examine specific frequency components, it is possible to plot a spatial topogram of the field which is found to correlate with a person's health status. Measurements are made from the front and the back of the body. In a person of good health, the aurogram field was regular and egg-shaped. In a sick person, substantial deformations were noted.

In New York's Bellevue Hospital the distinguished obstetrician and gynaecologist Dr. Louis Langman examined about 1,000 female patients with Dr. Burr's instruments and with his cooperation. The electrodes were placed on the cervix, and the ventral abdominal wall. In 102 cases, the abnormal voltage-gradient suggested the existence of malignancy. Subsequent surgical investigation confirmed that malignancy *did* exist in 95 out of the 102 women.

In another series of experiments, Dr. Langman discovered a correlation between voltage gradients and the depth of a hypnotic trance. This indicated that the mind could produce measurable changes in the body field.

The meridians of an acupuncture chart are awesome in their number and complexity. They have defied the efforts of researchers to discover a correlation between the so-called acupuncture points and, for example, nerve paths.

Dr. Victor Adamenko, a Russian scientist, and Dr. William Tiller, a physicist of the Material Sciences Department at Stanford University USA, have found that acupuncture points can be measured by simple apparatus designed to detect resistance.

If a person holds an electrode in one hand and runs the other hand over a person's body following the lines of acupuncture meridians, the resistance of the skin (normally one megohm) drops to 5% of this, i.e. 50,000 ohms.

Resistance differences occurred when a patient is in a state of illness. The more severe the illness, the greater the imbalance. Dr. Adamenko found a difference in measurable resistances both in the healer and the patient after a psychic healer had worked on the client in question. Acupuncture points can be stimulated in many mechanical ways by needles, pressure, etc., but Adamenko found that the best effects were through the efforts of psychic healers. In the case of Kirlian photography, discussed below, energy photographs of the acupuncture points show blobs of energy on the skin which vary in size with different diseases, a fact that offers enormous possibilities for studying the mechanisms involved in acupuncture as well as providing a useful means of diagnosis in its own right.

A number of experiments have shown conclusively the presence of an actual light surrounding the human body. In the 1950s Loebner introduced the first Optron detector in Europe. Light emitted from the human body was detected and amplified 100-fold by a selenium photoconductor connected to an electroluminescence display panel. Visible and ultraviolet light were found to be the main parts of the electromagnetic spectrum.

In 1954, the Italian researcher Colli first discovered that plants without special light-producing structures also emitted light spontaneously. In the 1960s Russian scientists showed that mammals also emitted such light and that the frequency of the light was in the visible region of the electromagnetic spectrum. Since the intensity of the light was about 100 times less than occurs in chemiluminescence, it was called 'dark luminescence'. Such ultra weak emissions were also shown to occur in the ultraviolet region by the Russian scientist Gurvich who first observed the phenomenon whilst dividing onion root cells.

Inushin, another Russian scientist, was able to detect emanations from the eyes of hypnotized subjects using film sensitive to ultra-violet.

The use of photomultiplier tubes has allowed scientists to localize ultraviolet emissions to the nucleus of the cell, although it appears that other parts of the cell also emit radiation of differing frequencies.

Konev, a Soviet scientist investigating cancer discovered that several hours before the initiation of cell division there was a dramatic increase in light emission. Evidence shows that rapidly dividing cells (associated with cancer) emit more light, although the detailed properties of this light as compared with similar emissions from normal cells is unknown.

German biophysicist F. A. Popp and his colleagues have done extensive investigations concerning ultra-weak emissions and cancer. Using photomultiplier tubes, they have shown that tumour biopsy specimens emit more light with different properties than is emitted from healthy tissues and have correlated such measurements with the degree of malignancy of a given tumour. One of the causes of cancer may be the alteration by foreign wave patterns which break up to indigenous bio-structure of the organism, but not everybody exposed to such agents develops cancer. Popp believes that each living cell has a standing wave field, which functions as a kind of defence system that wards off disturbing electromagnetic influences. The wave field also works as a carrier of biological information.

R. S. Stepanov has shown that there are significant differences between high frequency images obtained from cancerous cells, and images obtained by the same technique from normal cells. The authors claim that by using the Kirlian method the spread of *metastases* can be followed as well as the growth of the primary tumour.

American experience in aura investigation is considerable, though a major inhibiting factor is hostility from conservative medical practitioners and potential problems arising from the national habit of suing for damages at the slightest whim. In many states it is actually illegal to perform healing with the laying on of hands. In spite of this, some have the courage to stick their necks out. Among these was neuropsychiatrist Shafica Karagulla who worked with sensitives who could see the aura, and two of whom could see the chakras. This work can be read in her book *Breakthrough to Creativity, 1967.*

In New York in 1969, a group of physicists, physicians, electronic and biological specialists amalgamated their efforts forming the Energy Research Group (including Drs Richard Dobrin, Barbara Conway and John Pierrakos) with the aim of conducting a definitive study to determine whether the human energy field had a physical reality. It is worth noting that Dr. Pierrakos, a scientist and psychiatrist, had previously studied the energy fields of animals, crystals, plants and human beings clairvoyantly for a number of years, and was endeavouring to apply these observations in his practice. Pierrakos refers to a 'field phenomenon', a partial state analogous to the metabolism of the body with its mental state and physical activity. This 'field' is affected by humidity, ionization of the air and atmospheric conditions. He feels that we 'float' or 'swim' in this sea of energy which pulsates at the rate of between 15 and 25 times a minute in the average resting person. His findings received clairvoyantly broadly correspond with Kilner's findings, namely that there are pulsating levels of the aura around individuals which vary according to the state of health.

The Energy Research Group, using state of the art instrumentation, planned to observe the human body and to attempt to determine the relationship between the observed radiation and physical and emotional illness and health.

The method was as follows. Two photomultiplier tubes were placed in a light-tight room. This apparatus detects and amplifies low levels of light. The models were designed to respond to light in the visible and ultraviolet, but not in the infrared part of the spectrum. The apparatus would therefore exclude variations of the natural heat from the body. The subjects stood 16 inches from the tubes which were aimed at the abdomen.

With the subjects, an average light emission of 15% above the background noise was recorded. This low light level – in the range of 20–200 photons per second – is within the range of human night vision. However, 90% of individuals gave a recordable signal. A few individuals could increase the light emission by 100% simply by trying to activate their energy fields. The subjects claimed to be projecting energy from either their solar plexus, their heads or their hands. There was no perceptible increase in the temperature of the darkroom in these studies, which rules out the contribution of thermal noise.

Another strange phenomenon which was found repeatedly with strong subjects was the observation that the photomultiplier signal did not completely disappear when the subject left the darkroom. The signal decayed over a period of 15–20 minutes. This 'lag effect' has been observed by other investigators and has led to the postulation that some form of energy has been left in the room by the subject.

Meditation increased the intensity of the subject's signal. Strangely, intense thought reduced the field intensity. In another experiment, a pregnant woman was seated on the floor of the dark-room with her body out of range of visibility of the photomultiplier tubes. A large signal was nonetheless recorded as if she were project-ing or emitting a visible signal from her head and body. This effect supports the evidence for an emitted field. In other experiments, sub-jects were able to project their energy into the darkroom with visible increases in the observed signal.

The opposite type of effect was noted with several subjects, who decreased the observed signal below the ambient level when they entered the room. This included one agitated subject who appeared to draw energy from her surroundings. The subjective impression of the experimenters was that she was 'energy sucking' from the people that she came into contact with before and after the experi-mental run.

Attempts to video the signal resulted in the sight of a thin pulsat-ing field around the body. The signal was analysed and divided into 22 shades of grey. Each shade was given a different colour. This device ensured a higher degree of sensitivity than the human eye. Further, several horn-shaped structures were seen in areas corre-sponding to what eastern literature describes as the chakras, or open-ings into which energy flows into the body from the sea of energy that surrounds it.

All subjects were asked to place their hands together, and then to draw them apart slowly. Energy field lines were displayed joining the fingers together. This effect occurred for all subjects tested indepen-dently of the angle at which the hands were separated. During these recording sessions, persons who claimed to be able to see the aura vis-ibly recorded their observations on the sound track of the videotape. The TV monitor was not visible to these observers. The research groups found that about one third of the visual observations were vis-ible in the TV picture.

The group concluded that there was clear evidence for the human energy field and agrees with the descriptions of the field found in lit-erature. It was clear that the photomultiplier tubes were detecting only a small proportion of the energy field, and that there was scope to further examine the energy field with an image intensified televi-sion camera. It would then be possible to place narrow band filters

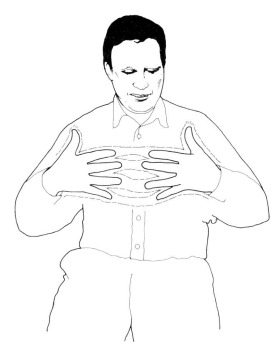

This is an experiment which can be performed by anyone. Sit quietly in a chair. Place your hands about 20 cm apart. Move your hands towards each other and then slightly from side to side. Do not 'think' about this action but concentrate on any feelings. You may feel prickles in the fingers of one or both hands. They will vary as you move your hands.

before the lens to further refine the observations of the frequency range of the aura.

There are many other types of experiment to show that matter has the power to influence other matter at a distance. In 1973, scientists at the State Medical School, and the School of Automatics and Electrometrics, Novosibirsk, U.S.S.R. experimented with distant interactions between two tissue cultures, one of which was infected by a toxic external agent. Various types of culture were taken, e.g. chicken embryos, divided into two and placed in isolated containers so designed to preserve optical 'contact' through quartz windows. The interactions between the cultures were determined by the number of cells killed (cytopathic). A 'mirror' cytopathic effect was observed in the tissue culture not exposed to the toxic agent. Using a total of 1,785 samples of which 1,327 were controls, a total of 458 samples were infected with viruses and poison agents. In 76% of the cases, cross-infections were noted. This 'mirror' effect occurred whether the external agent was a virus, a chemical, or a lethal amount of ultraviolet radiation.

The experiment only worked with thin quartz glass, and the optical contact needed to be at least four hours in duration; the experiments needed to take place in total darkness.

This cross-infection may be due to information transmitted from one tissue culture to the other by means of a bio-luminescent code. Infrared and ultraviolet photons can pass through quartz glass but not through ordinary glass.

Additional experiments with a sensitive photomultiplier tube (which records photon flow) revealed a change in nature of the flow when the culture was infected with toxic materials. First the photon flow surged, then stopped, then surged again, then stopped. Each of the three viruses used produced these four stages to some degree. It is important to note that a virus passes through four stages when infecting a cell. First it penetrates the cell wall, then sheds its protein sheath, then directs the cell to produce new viruses which soon burst forth from the cell. It is possible that the infected cells communicated to the non-infected cells 'coded' information about their condition through the flow of photons. Further experiments showed that the photon flow was ultraviolet rather than infrared. Differences in emission of from eight to twelve times was noted, and the effect lasted for up to eighteen hours.

The mechanism of information transmission is certainly mysterious. Two groups of American scientists researched on the ability of plants to emit signals which are picked up by other plants. In the 1970s Dr. Gordon Orians and Dr. Rhoades, two biologists at the University of Washington, set out how trees survive mass attacks by insects. They placed swarms of as many as 700 caterpillars and webworms in the branches of dozens of willows and alders to see what kinds of defence mechanism the trees might place against the attack. The trees began altering the chemistry of their leaves to make them less palatable and nutritious to the insects. They began to form protein in such a way as to make it indigestible. As a result, some insect invaders were starving and even dying from protein deficiency.

The predators could neither resist the cold weather, or ordinary bacteria.

This was remarkable enough, but what really stunned the botanical biologists was that nearby trees of the same species suddenly began to mount the same chemical defences even though they had not been invaded by the insects.

They eliminated transmission by the tree roots by chemical examination, and noted that some of the trees that responded to the fraternal warning were 200ft from the attacked trees. Was this a transmission of an airborne chemical or was it an electromagnetically radiated signal? By coincidence, at Dartmouth College, New Hampshire, Dr. Jack Schultz, a biologist and Dr. Ian Baldwin, a chemist, were getting similar results in experiments with sugar maples and poplar seedlings.

The idea of transmission of energy itself is not new. Michael Faraday concluded that every single atom influences all other atoms, i.e. the whole universe. The notion of the interconnectedness of things was expounded not only by the great religious thinkers and Greek philosophers such as Socrates and Plato, but modern thinkers like Jung and Einstein.

Another example is the now famous '100 monkey' effect. In the 1950s on the Island of Koshima, researchers observing the local macaque monkeys used to put sweet potatoes on the beach for them. The monkeys ate the potatoes, sand and all. One day a monkey genius discovered she could clean the potatoes by washing them in the sea. Soon others followed her example until all the monkeys (100 of them) adopted this new technique. On nearby islands, researchers conducting the same experiment reported that all their monkeys started to use this same technique. To the scientists this was quite remarkable and has become known as the '100 monkey effect'. This lends weight to the theory that each species has a type of informational web that operates across both space and time to which individual members are attuned.

An Icelandic science pioneer in the early part of this century, Dr. Helgi Pjeturss (1873–1949), gives us a visionary statement.

> "*Every single movement that occurs in the universe, every single particle that exists, endeavours to reproduce itself throughout the whole universe. It attempts to bring the whole*

universe into harmony with itself. From every being, the largest and the most complicated one to the smallest and the most uniform one, there proceeds a radiation that aims at the reproduction of that being."

It is clear that he does not see bio-radiation as a factor apart from nature or beyond the reach of physics, but just as a kind of extension of the inorganic forces, part of the realm of nature which has different characteristics and features.

There seems no limit to the subject matter and the possible modality of transmission between so-called discrete entities. In the universe there are at least seven different levels of substance and these different substances are configured differently. They obey different kinds of laws – unique types of laws – and they have unique characteristics of radiation (absorption and emission). From evidence, they appear to operate in different kinds of space-time frames and are distinct from each other.

They can be defined as follows: the physical level – the coarsest; the etheric level (the Soviets call this the bioplasmic body or energy body), some call it the pre-physical body, the astral level; the instinctive or territorial mind level; the intellectual mind; the spiritual or higher mind; and finally the spirit or soul of the individual. These layers interpenetrate each other in nature and may interact with each other. We can remember the metaphysical principle:

As above, so below; as below, so above.

If you imagine a number of pieces of glass placed upon each other, each with different patterns drawn on them with different coloured inks, and look through them, the light that can shine through depends on the nature and configuration of the patterns. If one layer is 90% opaque, then light cannot shine through. The level at which the opaqueness happens is not relevant; it's the sum total effect that matters.

We can relate the physical level to order or chaos; the pre-physical level to the organization of matter, as with Harold Saxton Burr's discoveries of thought and organizing fields; the other levels are characterized by magnetic fields, and the phenomenon called the 'aura'.

We use the phrase 'the light shone out of their eyes' or 'she went round in a black mood all day' or 'he saw red'. This is surely an indication of the subconscious awareness of this incredible matrix of forces that surround us and are controlled or influenced by our free will. It is most difficult to track back a physical process for any roots in the non-physical. The question is 'What causes what?' Does life cause fields or do fields cause life? Is the universe more like a great thought than a great machine?

~2~

The mysterious phenomenon of Kirlian Photography

Some would say after a cursory glance that Kirlian is no more than a product of the electrical discharge of a current through the hands. Bearing in mind the nature and subtlety of the phenomena referred to in the previous chapter, this might be seen to be a rather brave assumption.

What is a mystery? Regarded as hidden or inexplicable matter, the word itself is derived from the Greek word *muo*, closed lips or eyes. This explains why a theologian might describe a mystery as an aspect of God's universe which may never be understood by our finite mind and should not be tampered with. On the other hand, some scientists would define mystery as that which has not yet been explained but with the march of time will be understood. Certainly the idea of a mystery is often used in the popular mind to justify the building of support for hypothesis, fantastic or not, and engage in systematic correlations of facts and perceptions. For example 'Has Earth in the past been visited by intelligent beings from the region of the star Sirius?'; 'The mystery of rocks in death valley that move by themselves'. It is only scientists with a vision, such as Albert Einstein, who had open minds that would never be closed to such mysteries.

In the face of events which are outside the range of our comprehension, are we being asked to suspend our rational mind and humbly accept that we are ignorant? Or does our rational mind have a duty to de-mystify the mystery, to refuse to accept any phenomenon outside our knowledge until it is somehow tamed and brought into order? It is this latter which can not only prevent the gullible being misdirected, but can also prevent or delay the acceptance of material which could advance mankind's vision of who he is. We will do ourselves a service if we view Kirlian with a dispassionate but kindly eye.

Reductionistic thinking has no place in a matter which straddles so many disciplines and which requires, at the very least, lateral thinking of a high order. With these thoughts in the background, let us turn to the topic of energetic photography itself.

We have seen that living things are surrounded by a wide variety of phenomena. Let's have a look at these via the photographic phenomenon nicknamed Kirlian Photography but which should more accurately be called 'corona discharge photography'.

'Curious patterns' associated with high voltages were obtained in the middle of the eighteenth century when an experimenter named Carsten recorded the phenomenon of 'electric patterns' produced by a coin on a metal plate.

The most thorough research into the basic phenomenon of corona discharge photography was made by a Yakub Narkevitch Yokdo who was born about 1850 into a Polish noble family in the region of Minsk in Russia. A widely educated man, his work on electrography included the observation that pictures from a healthy person were different from those from a sick person, and he recorded differences between people tired or excited, sleeping or awake. He drew attention to the possible use of this discipline in determining psychological compatibility. Regrettably, his records and his instruments were lost during the Russian revolution.

In 1886 the French investigator, Henri Baraduc, using a Wimshurst machine took photographs of human hands and leaves

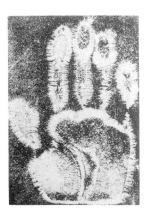

An early example of an electrically generated pattern around the hands

which captured, as he claimed, "the lights of the human soul".

In 1889 a Czech physicist, Professor Batholomew Navratil, described a "new kind of electric pattern" made visible by electrophotography, a word first coined by him. Later, in 1911, he presented a full technical paper.

In 1884 the famous Serbian Nikola Tesla arrived in the USA. After a period with the Edison Company in New Jersey he formed his own company and developed the coil which bears his name. He conducted many experiments with high-voltage photography and demonstrated by means of electric fields how to light 200 lamps at a distance of 25 miles.

The research carried out by Tesla with high tension transformers showed that luminous discharges appear around the body when it is exposed to powerful high frequency electromagnetic fields. Tesla was one of the first people to use high-frequency high-voltage fields to expose film and photographic paper. He also built the first alternating-current motor, AC generator, high-frequency coil, and transformer.

In 1896 Yakub Narkevitch-Yodko, an engineer and electrical researcher, exhibited "electrographic photographs obtained with the help of quiet electrical discharges" at a meeting of the Russian Technical Society. This was only a couple of years after the discovery of X-rays by the German physicist Roentgen, or Wurzburg, and many laboratories were experimenting with electrical discharge apparatus.

In the 1920s Albert Nodon produced the first spontaneous radiographs which appeared on ordinary photographic paper without electrical stimulus, thus requiring several hours of exposure.

In the early 1900s, Dr. E. F. Strong of Tufts University Medical School, USA, likewise used a Tesla-type coil to produce electrophotographs of his hand. However, in general, the most innovatory work in this type of photography originated from Russia. This is partly because the ideas of Tesla and other inventors were taken seriously there.

Renewed interest was shown in corona discharge photography itself in the 1930s by Drs Pratt and Schlemmer at Charles University in Prague. Their findings were published in the *Journal of the Biological Photographic Association* which describes their experiments using living tissues rather than metals. Their definition, "Electrography consists of making contact prints of various objects placed on the photographic emulsion in an electrical field during the electric discharges" is a definition that is still useful today.

Decades after the first experiments, the husband and wife team who popularized the concept of high voltage photography appeared on the scene. The Russian husband and wife team, Semyon and Valentina Kirlian, gave their name to this phenomenon. They lived in the town of Krasnodar in the Ukraine. Semyon was an electrical and mechanical Jack of all trades. One day in 1939 he was engaged in some repair work on a high-voltage machine when he noticed a spark jump between the machine and his hand. His unfailing curiosity led him to wonder what would happen if a sheet of photo-sensitive material were placed in the path of this spark. The resulting streamer-like pattern prompted him on a path of discovery that was to last the rest of his life. In a further refinement he was able to monitor this luminescence on a continuous basis.

Semyon and Valentina Kirlian

The result, as Semyon described it, was "the most fantastic scene" they had ever witnessed. The hand was transformed into a display of lights, flares, sparks and twinkling effects in a constant movement of glorious colour. Some lights appeared to be moving, while others pulsated; parts of the hand showed cloudy patches, but the whole appeared as a firework display with the physical hand seen dimly in the background. The impression was of a giant computer screen constantly adjusting to a read-out. His visionary side was inspired to conclude that this phenomenon "touched a whole new world of possibilities".

Two specific classes of response were noted by the Kirlians.

1. The effect from non-living objects was repeatable using the same equipment with the same settings.
2. The effect from all living matter was variable and non-repeatable, even with the same equipment and setting.

Semyon and his wife worked for a 20-year period in a small two-room apartment which was their home. They became convinced that this 'inner body' of light reflected the state of well being – or otherwise – of the physical body. One of their breakthroughs came when they photographed two apparently identical leaves, one of which gave the expected aura, while the other appeared dull and lifeless. The donor of the leaves then explained that the first leaf was from a

Picture of leaf a) intact b) shortly after cutting and c) five minutes later. Notice the change in shape of the surrounding energy pattern.

healthy plant whereas the other was from a plant contaminated by poison. It appeared from this experiment that the Kirlians could predict that disease or death was imminent. Eventually the Kirlians came to realize that this second 'inner body', the aura, is a whole unified organism in itself, possibly manifesting its own unique range of bio-energetic fields.

Semyon Kirlian, working with the Krasnodar surgeon, Ruben Stepanov, took corona discharge photographs of samples of stomach tissue taken from 166 patients, some of whom had cancer of the stomach, while the rest had other gastric diseases. They found that the tissue from the cancer patients produced many tiny white and grey spots on the photograph, whereas the non-cancerous tissue produced large well-defined spots. Even at this early stage the practical benefits of this method of diagnosis became obvious; the diagnosis could be made in 15 minutes compared with several days required for an equivalent histological diagnosis.

This collection of observations and data dubbed Kirlian Photography, though impressive, remained without scientific use, and only came to the attention of researchers from the west who, in 1959, started to investigate it as a topic of scientific studies. World-wide study could have started much earlier but the Kirlians could not publish the results of their work because for purely bureaucratic reasons corona discharge photography was classified as secret by the then Soviet government.

In 1949 the first patent for the invention was taken out by S. D. Kirlian and Valentina Kirlian, and in 1964 the phenomenon was presented under the description: 'High frequency, high voltage photography' (Kirlian & Kirlian 1961). Kirlian's first scientific report was co-authored by his wife, and appeared in the *Russian Journal of Scientific and Applied Photography and Cinema Photography* in 1961. The Kirlians described their method as "one of transformation of non-electric phenomena of living and non-living nature into electrical phenomena" (Kirlian & Kirlian 1961). An article about the Kirlians' work was published in 1964 in the periodical *Soviet World*, which started to bring high-frequency photography to the attention of the Western world. One of the earliest reported phenomena was the 'phantom leaf' experiment where a Kirlian photograph of a leaf was made before and after cutting off a section. It was noted that the outline of the whole leaf remained, though the physical leaf had been dissected. This could not be explained by the exudation of water droplets since the outline pattern was regular. Scientists considered the cause of this 'ghost' to be a form of energy, which may have its origin in electrical activity or electromagnetic fields but could be considered a different sort of matter – plasma; streams of masses or ionized particles. Here was evidence that there is an energy matrix in all living things, an invisible body penetrating our physical bodies. Experiments have also shown that the corona of a leaf can be restored by being held for a few minutes in the hand of a healer.

 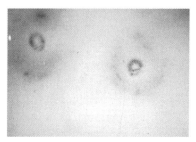

Grains of wheat with an identical appearance (left) *fertile and* (right) *infertile as subsequent planting proved.*

The same piece of bread as a control (left) *and after being touched for a few seconds by a healer* (right).

In the 1960s a group of scientists from the Kirov State University of Kazakhstan in Alma-Ata subjected the Kirlian process to an electron microscope to examine the high-frequency discharge. They saw a living 'double' of the living organism, which was not a chaotic system but a living entity in itself. In 1968 a group of doctors led by Dr. Victor Inushin announced that all living things – plants, animals and humans – have a counterpart body of energy, which they christened the "Biological Plasma Body". They considered that the bio-luminescence of the Kirlian photos was caused by the bio-plasma, not the electrical state of the organism. This biological plasma is specific for every organism, tissue and possibly bio-molecule.

However, Kirlian Photography first came to the notice of the West in 1970, when energy pictures of phantom leaves were published in a book by journalists Ostrander and Schroeder entitled *Psychic Discoveries behind the Iron Curtain*. Kirlian photography's impact was reinforced in the USA in 1972 with a conference on Kirlian Photography, Acupuncture and the Human Aura held in New York.

By the time of the Second International Conference of the Union for Medical and Applied Bio-Electrography in London in 1990, bio-electrographic images were being utilized in a wide variety of ways. At this conference the trend of interest in Kirlian became clearer; more were interested in the practical applications of Kirlian than in the fundamental physics.

These are some of the hundreds of applications that Kirlian photography has been used for:

1.   Measuring the life-force in seeds and plants;
2.   Detecting illness before physical symptoms appear;
3.   For use in conjunction with other therapies such as acupuncture, homoeopathy and spiritual healing, as a cross check to the effectiveness of the methods;
4.   To investigate the residual toxic effects of drug addiction;
5.   To evaluate the effect of parental conflict on children;
6.   To assess psychological compatibility between two people;
7.   To evaluate the ability of a therapist to activate the self-healing processes in a patient.

Some indication of scientific interest in a phenomenon can be gained from an analysis of published papers. According to Gordon Gadsby, a summary of whose work appears further on, 635 references were found in database searches dated thus:

Pre 1970	=	33	i.e. 5% of total
1970–79	=	492	i.e. 77.5% of total
1980–90	=	110	i.e. 17.5% of total

Thousands of researchers and hundreds of different machines have found one thing in common – a strange series of patterns which radiate not only from human beings, but plants, and even stones and crystals.

The mounting body of evidence – partly produced by scientists – means that study or acknowledgement of these phenomena does not require committing intellectual suicide. We can choose from a vast array of research work to give us some indication of the widespread possibilities of the Kirlian method.

S. Mallikarjun, writing in the *Journal of the International Kirlian Research Association* in 1986, investigated the thumb prints of cancer patients. Results indicated that while Kirlian photographs from fingers of healthy subjects showed cyclic changes, in cancer patients intense luminosity was found with no cyclic change.

Earlier, in the 1970s, Dr. Ion Dumitrescu working in Romania used Kirlian techniques to screen 6,000 patients. He claimed a 100% success rate in the early detection of breast cancer and 74% of the total cases of malignancy. In three cases of sarcoma the Kirlian image showed the tumour whereas the X-rays were normal.

Dr. Ramesh Singh Chouhan is a research office from Pondicharry, India who has devoted his whole life to the study of Kirlian photography, and at the 1990 conference in London he explained his stance on Kirlian in particular and cooperation with scientists in general:

> *"In order to communicate with scientists and to attract grants, we must use their language. Use their terminology.*
>
> *Lack of voltage and frequency controls can put off scientists. We have developed a glass electrode which enables us to see the picture in real time. We wanted to do away with subjective analysis and use digitization and computerisation. What is necessary for something to be accepted is objectivity and scientific protocol. I do not deny the need for human emotions; the need to be involved with the patients.*
>
> *There are two levels of variation in the emissions; day to day ups and downs, and gross variations. It is important to take many photographs and seek out the trends. Ultimately when we do statistical analysis of the images, how likely is it that the patterns would have arisen through chance?"*

They examined 1,500 female individuals in a double blind study. 'Double blind' means that the person doing the testing was not aware of what sort of the problem the patient had. The subjects were then clinically examined and the tissues were biopsied and a histopathological examination was done.

The clinician was not aware of the results of his own testing and the Kirlian photographer was not aware of the results of the clinician or the histopathologist. The results from the clinician, the Kirlian researcher and the histopathologist were compared.

Of the 1,500 subjects, clinically positive for cancer malignancy was 1,178, histopathologically was 1,049, and bio-electrographically was 1,066. Negative for cancer, or normal evaluation were thus recorded: clinically 322; histopathologically 451; bioelectrographically 334. When we matched the cases we found that 1,006 were positive using all three types of measurement, 254 were negative using all three criteria. This means that there was an 84% correlation of all the three parameters in this double blind study.

In addition we had	clinical	histopathological	Kirlian
	68–	18+	50–

11% false positives for bio-electrography. The Kirlian findings could not be corroborated by either of the other two studies.

These were the number of cases in which findings of malignancy, clinically and histologically, could not be corroborated by the Kirlian electrographical method

25	25	0

This false negative result amounted to 1.67%. This is significant in terms of reliability testing of the histology and Kirlian method, we found that in histology, 24.9% were false negatives vs 1.67% false negative in the case of the Kirlian photographs. This shows that Kirlian photography is a much better way of screening and diagnosing as far as cancer is concerned. Also, 30% of the subjects were negative up to 12 months before diagnosis. Of the 12% of 'false positives', 57% of the 12% were proved to be positive within a nine month period. This means that Kirlian can detect the disease in a pre-malignant condition. This is an example of where scientific methodology in conjunction with Kirlian photography can make a significant contribution to fighting disease.

There is a need to do some fundamental research. The increased radiation or luminosity in cancer conditions is due to the tumour currents, because we know that tumours function as batteries. They do generate electrical currents. We found alternating currents at about 100 MHz which are maximal mitosis due to the large amount of cell division.

When the ancients said that we are luminaries, they were in effect saying that any living thing is a walking candle. As we have seen from photon experiments, the human body is giving off a few hundred photons per square centimetre every second. The benefits of using Kirlian for cancer screening is that this method is absolutely non-invasive, gives very early indication, with very high reliability even at a single sample, low false negatives, useful as a monitor during treatment.

There is no current method of knowing if chemotherapy or radiation or surgery has done any good to the patient unless we wait for some time to see the symptoms. In the radiation therapy you do not know if the symptoms produced by the patient are due to radiation sickness or because of the increased or speeded up processes of cancer. The Kirlian method has found changes arising from the injection of chemotherapeutic agents within one hour. The researchers found that if chemotherapy was inappropriate, the image size either did not respond or increased.

In the case of biopsy, three days are required to be sure about the test; in the case of Kirlian, only 30 minutes were required and this at very low cost. Due to this, the test could be a sentinel on a regular basis. Chouhan also studied induced cancer regression not using chemotherapeutic agents or radiation but using micro-electric currents. The process itself is based on micro-electric currents and consists of wiring up the tumour to a current source and causing a regression of the delinquent cells. Rehabilitation of the delinquent cancer cells is a more intelligent method than destroying them with radiation. This again can be monitored by Kirlian.

From the electrical point of view, Chouhan's studies showed a change in the electrical conductivity of the skin, not just in the region of the cancer, but in all parts of the body. An effect anywhere is instantly responded to by the body as a whole. Nothing can be isolated.

In the 1973 issue of *Medical News* in the USA, two MDs, Dr. Michael Shakter and Dr. David Sheinkin who were psychiatrists at the Rockland County Community Health Centre in Ponoma, New York State, reported on their investigation of the medical potential of Kirlian Photography. They sought a correlation between the finger-pad corona patterns and the type of psychiatric problem encountered. With patients suffering from schizophrenia they found a lack of clarity in the fingerpad corona. Treatment with suitable medication was given and in about a week the fingerpad photos improved in clarity. Patterns associated with problems which were mainly physical such as pneumonia, gastroenteritis and upper respiratory infection were completely different in nature. The article suggested that it may be possible to predict the onset of such episodes by monitoring changes in fingertip corona.

Professors Murstein and Hadjoliam reported in the September 1975 issue of *Human Behaviour* a positive correlation between aura size and attraction. A positive attraction will show an increase in the diameter of the corona discharge and similarly a dislike will produce a decrease in corona size.

In the early 1980s an Athens doctor of psychiatry, Vittoria Marangoni, analysed 120 subjects, half of them controls and half of them severely psychotic in-patients. The research was conducted in the State Psychiatric Hospital in Athens. Using a double blind method of analysis, images were taken using black and white pictures. The Kirlian pictures of the psychotics showed highly disruptive patterns of the corona images; the patterns of the controls were well organized and uniform. The differences were significant at the 0.0001 level of confidence.

In the second stage of the research, a linear study of selected patients was carried out. The disputed patterns of the patients in the acute phase of their illness showed normalization of the patterns after only one or two days of the correct (for the patient) drug; no changes were seen when an inappropriate drug for the patient was given, no matter how much the dosage was increased. Also it was possible to detect when the patients did not comply with the treatment and secretly threw away the medication or, even when taking the medication, they were going to relapse. The doctor monitored one patient over a period of one month. The patient was doing very well. He was working, taking his medicine and was even painting. He asked if he could discontinue the medication. The doctor decided to make a decision after viewing another Kirlian picture and was puzzled to note that it showed great instability. Three days later the patient had a terrible relapse and tried to kill himself.

A further more detailed study involved three groups of 12 subjects each. One of the groups was of normal controls, one of psychotic out-patients, and one of neurotics. The normality of the controls was documented by MMPI profile. To all the subjects, a psychiatrist administered the Hamilton anxiety scale, clinical Global Impression scale and another test for schizophrenia. At the same time, Kirlian pictures were taken. Colour positive film plates were used – in this case Kodak ectachrome 4" × 5" tungsten. In the method used, blue and red colours predominated. Whereas with normal subjects the complete blue corona showed round the fingertip, in psychotic subjects the team found no blue but a pervasive dark red band round the hand; the corona was without streamers. In neurotic patients, the predominant colour was red; the streamers were chaotic, turning on themselves as if being blown in the wind. In the statistical analysis, a significant inverse predominance of blue was found to correlate with low mean scores in pathology. Dr. Marangoni concludes:

> *"In the study of over 1,000 Kirlian photos I am convinced that Kirlian photography can be a very sensitive index in psycho-pathological changes. I don't know if these images are specific or not. Maybe they are only general indexes of disease imbalance, of suffering of the many bodies that we have. Scientists and medical doctors should help us to find out the deep true mechanism of the phenomena."*

The above examples are a brief description of a series of discoveries which will hopefully have a far greater influence on our thinking in medicine and psychology as time goes by.

We can therefore conclude from material in the preceding chapters:

1.   The human body has an electrical aspect, part of which is reflected in a 'field' effect, not only within it but at a distance from it.

2.   This electrical matrix is affected by the physical and mental state of the subject and changes accordingly.

3.   The characteristics can be measured by standard electrical measuring apparatus including high impedance voltmeters.

4.   The human body radiates light, which varies according to the psychological and physical condition of the body.

5.   If the body is placed within the ambit of a high frequency field and a sheet of photo-sensitive material is interposed, various patterns are obtained which may be due to a combination of the physical, mental and psychological state of the subject.

Leonard Konikiewitz of the Polyclinic Medical Centre, Harrisburg, and Benjamin Shafiroff of the New York College of Medicine studied the menstrual cycle stages of 30 women in 1978 using Kirlian photography. Each corona discharge of the thumb was examined for shape, luminosity and streamer formation.

A total of 30 women ranging from 20 years to 42 years took part in the study extending over a minimum period of two menstrual cycles. Fourteen women served as controls; 5 women taking contraceptive medication; five women in their menopause; four pre-pubetal girls. No change in corona pattern was noted in the control groups, but with the subjects corona discharge patterns taken during menses were generally weak and ill-defined; luminosity, corona and streamers increased in intensity and in numbers as the Graafian follicle approached full development. The corona discharge image became developed maximally at the time of rupture of the follicle and continued with varying degree of intensity through the ovulatory phase. During the period of luteinization the corona image slowly decreased in intensity so that when menstruation appeared the image was at its lowest developmental stage. The researchers concluded that fingertip electrographs may prove to be an effective non-invasive means of monitoring the four stages that comprise the menstrual cycle.

The use of Kirlian photography within acupuncture provides qualitative information about the Chinese meridian system. The Kirlian photograph registers the energy emissions from the fingers and toes and gives a detailed picture of meridian energy. For an

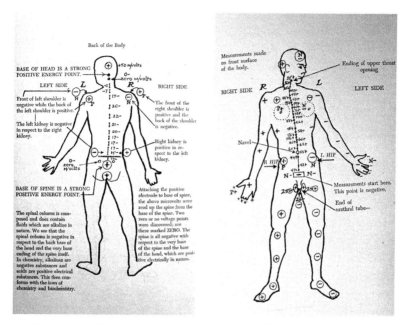

*Schematic diagrams of acupuncture meridians from the front
and the back*

acupuncturist, the most significant points for treating are the 'Master
Points' or 'End Points' which are 1/12th of an inch from the finger-
nails. Members of the Equinox group of biophysical practitioners
have been using Kirlian diagnostic techniques for many years and
have processed thousands of photographs. By cross-referencing
Kirlian photographs with basic electrical resistance measurements, it
has been found that dense images on the photograph correlate with
high resistance measurements – typical of degenerative conditions
such as osteoarthritis. Faint Kirlian photographs do not usually
denote deficiency of energy but emissions at the red wavelengths,
which do not react with black and white photographic emulsions, e.g.
allergic conditions such as asthma. These images are characteristic of
inflammatory conditions and low resistance readings.

A recent study by Gordon Gadsby entailed taking a random
selection of one hundred Kirlian photographs from his records and
submitting them to an extensive statistical analysis.

All the Kirlian photographs were taken with an Equinox Mark I
camera using a voltage of 20KV, a frequency of 50Hz, a pulse repeti-

tion frequency of 250/second, a peak current at 9.5mA on the foot setting and 5mA on the hand setting with a pre-set exposure time of 6 seconds and 2 seconds respectively. The camera pulse trains were interleaved, i.e. the left hand plate pulsed positively, then the right hand plate, then the left hand plate again alternately. All the photographs were taken on Agfa Rapitone P1–1 paper and manually developed with Agfa G170c developer and G386 fixer by the same operator in order to maintain a consistency of method.

It had been anticipated, before the study, that the strength of the relationships between the electrical resistance readings and the Kirlian Index scores, would have been considerably higher than the study found. The positive correlation of the hands was expected but a negative correlation of the feet confounded the proposed model. It may therefore be too easy to take a single photograph which elegantly explains the patient's illness and then to infer that other diagnostic Kirlian photographs may do likewise (see examples): this study suggests that we cannot make this observation routinely in the light of our current knowledge.

Normally the hands and feet are used by Kirlian researchers to determine states of health. However, Alfred Benjamin, a Medical Photographer working out of the Polyclinic Medical Centre in the mid 1980s, used high voltage in a slightly different application. He investigated differential reactions of normal and pathologic cells using blood spots. A blood sample was placed on a layer of voltage sensitive liquid crystals and earthed via a grounding wire. A high-voltage high-frequency current was passed through the circuit, and an electronic flash probe was used to record the effects as they occurred. Observations indicated a differential in the decay rate and characteristics of the crystals between cancerous and normal patients.

Ion Dumitrescu, a Romanian medical doctor with a degree in electronics, started his own research from Semyon Kirlian's work. He investigated over 5,000 normal healthy human beings as well as 171 who were suffering from malignant tumours in different parts of their bodies. He confirmed the locality of the tumours by electrographic methods in 74% of the cases.

Many interesting discoveries are awaiting the influence of one quality – creative imagination. If I had ignored my instinct and concentrated on single fingertips, I would have missed out on a whole bevy of vital clues. It is regrettable that those who are furthest advanced – the Russians – are the most under funded and largely inaccessible. With the rise in interest in all things paranormal (even to the extent of a specialist Russian TV channel!) the pace is set to hot up.

~3~

What is the Kirlian apparatus and how does it work?

Valentina and Semyon Kirlian gave their name to this unconventional form of photography in the way the brand name Hoover gave its name to vacuum cleaners. We 'hoover' the floor. We make a 'Kirlian' print. Kirlian photography, incidentally, is also known as corona discharge photography, bio-electro photography or electrodynamic imaging.

Kirlian photography has little in common with conventional photography. A sheet of film or paper is exposed, not optically through a system of lenses, but by placing the object to be photographed in contact with an electrostatic field. When any object – organic or inorganic – is placed in the stream of charged particles, the object is excited and a corona discharge takes place. Photosensitive materials contain silver halide in the emulsion layers. Silver halide is particularly sensitive to ultraviolet light.

Original Kirlian machine, the Verograph
Designed by Ted Van Der Veer, Holland.

The Kirlian machine itself comes in two parts. One contains the high voltage plate which is separated from the person by a layer of plastic insulation. Power is supplied by a small electric generator. The plate unit contains a high voltage transformer, similar to a car ignition coil.

To make a picture, it is important to follow the same routine. Place the left hand on the left side of the photo paper. 'Unroll' the hand on to the paper starting at the bottom. This ensures that the

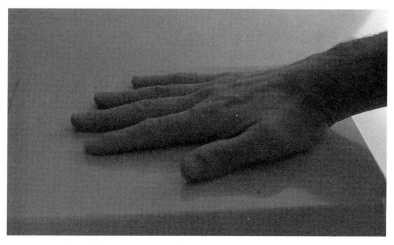

A hand being put on the machine in the correct way

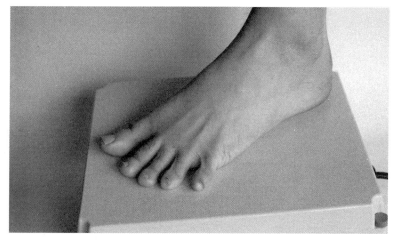

A foot being put on the machine

skin presents itself in a regular fashion to the paper, and that there-fore any anomalies are due to aberrations in the field pattern.

After the exposure, place the right hand on, whilst removing the left hand. This ensures regularity of position.

The Kirlian machine generates many thousands of volts but of necessity and for safety at a low current, approximately 10 milliamps. The charge goes from the machine to earth via the object being pho-tographed, utilizing its natural capacity to earth. In human subjects there is sufficient natural leakage to enable the required current to flow. A direct connection to earth via a wire or rod is sometimes used, but this is mainly required in the case of small, inanimate objects such as coins.

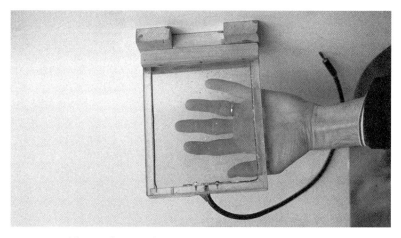

It is possible to observe the emanations in real time. A construction of two sheets of glass between which saline solution is poured. The electrode is placed in contact with the saline solution. In a darkened room the emanation can be clearly seen.

What is happening during the exposure? In effect, the current is say-ing 'I need to discharge to earth, what is the path of least resistance?' It's rather like water finding its way over a cliff forming a waterfall. If the human body says, in effect, 'Oh no you don't. I am going to resist you' then a continuous inner corona is formed. If the field is not harmonious then the streamers will be wavy. If the body field can only resist in part the external static field, then there will be holes in the corona.

The choice that the discharge takes depends on the nature of the electrical 'terrain' or the static field surrounding the object or person.

Schematic model of the machine. At the top, the hand. Underneath a sheet of photo paper. Under that the plastic cover of the machine, under that a metal sheet to which the high voltage is applied

Whilst there is very little difference between exposures taken at intervals of stones or plants, there is a considerable variation between a series of photos taken of human individuals. A hand or foot can have no photo, or a florid photo. The left hand can show, but not the right hand. Bits of the corona can be missing, misshapen, containing anomalies such as balls of light.

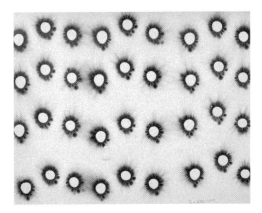

*Examples of fingertips taken at five second intervals.
Note variations in the plumes of energy.*

Exposures have to be made in a dark room free from all light in the case of colour photography. This includes the red indicator lamp on the Kirlian machine! In the case of black and white photography, a red safe light can be used. The relevant paper or film is not sensitive to light at the infra-red end of the spectrum.

As an added precaution, any influence of electromagnetic field radiations from other individuals or any electrical wire bearing current has to be taken into consideration. Thus any electrical apparatus and the operator himself needs to be at least two metres from the subject. The room itself, therefore, needs to be of reasonable size and well ventilated to ensure that the exposure only reflects the characteristics of the subject.

This book is not designed to be a manual for aspiring experimenters but a discussion of the principles which pertain to this discipline. Nevertheless, experimenters are strongly advised to follow the health and safety instructions issued by the manufacturers of the equipment and the chemicals they use.

What parts of the body are best suited to be photographed?

The single most interesting area is the hand. One reason is that the hand is among the most 'well informed' organs in terms of the abundance of nervous tissue. The thumb, incidentally, has as many nerve endings as all the rest put together. There are rich connections between the brain and other parts of the body, not only for the flow of sensory information but coordination. The two main areas being the mouth and the hands.

Right from the start of research into the Kirlian phenomena, the tradition has been to photograph the fingertips. With the exception of Dumitrescu, the Russian and American work concentrated on one finger – usually the index finger – and made that print the basis for analysis.

Notable are the German researcher Mandal and others who correlate the results with acupuncture, so called 'terminal point diagnosis'. This method is undoubtedly successful within its own parameters. My own contribution to the field was to examine the radiation from the whole hand. Why did I chose the whole hand? In retrospect I could think up all sorts of plausible grounds, but in fact at the time it seemed the obvious thing to do. Surely, I thought, the bigger the area the more information would be received. I suppose it was the same kind of instinct that would make me want to look at a map of

England as a background to a tour by motor car. Yes, the fingers may or may not give us information but what is the overall context of this. Does a flower grow in a desert or in a garden?

I now appreciate the logic that the area of the whole hand presented to a high frequency field is a much greater challenge for the body energy. In other words a larger area is a much greater test for the integrity of the energy body. From a purely practical point of view, hands happen to be more readily accessible as subjects, especially when the method is being demonstrated in a public place with a large through-put of people. All photographs are valid but the hands and the feet being rich in nervous tissue and in acupuncture points yield images that are particularly differentiated and therefore useful. In addition, whereas all parts of living tissue produce images of a sort, the difference in information received from the hands or feet compared with, say, the arm are equivalent to the differences between a busy railway junction and a rural line. Many more interchanges happen at the junction and therefore many more deductions can be made about the flow of 'traffic' which are more telling. This analogy can apply to the body condition which can thus be more perceptively analysed.

People often ask if it is necessary to be an expert in Kirlian photography to benefit others. In a word, no. The main requirement is a determination to carefully observe and monitor all experiments. It is also useful to combine Kirlian with another discipline such as healing, acupuncture, etc. All potential users of the equipment should at the very least learn to make records every time a photo is made. This comprises what we call the 'scientific method'. All experiments need to be replicable. This means that if someone else comes along expressing interest, you can tell them what you did, the state of the client at the time, what if anything happened between the making of the first photograph and subsequent photographs. This is especially important for acupuncturists, healers, counsellors, etc., and also when before and after photos are made on a number of occasions. Never throw away examples which did not make sense. They will often do so later! Write on the back of the photo what you did, or write a number on and attach a form to it.

No one is precluded from making an important discovery. There is no law saying that only those with letters after their name can make meaningful correlations or deductions.

Remember that acupuncture may have been discovered by accident when, so legend tells us, soldiers found that the act of twisting and pulling out arrows from victims resulted in the lessening of pain. There are thousands of 'unqualified' healers, helpers, comforters who achieve more in real terms than many in the medical profession. They themselves would be the first to admit that the mechanisms are not understood. Do not be put off by sceptics and cynics. They contribute very little to the sum total of human knowledge. In many cases they have a deliberately limited view of holistic diagnosis and in virtually all cases that they have not tried the method for themselves. Follow your instinct. It is a good idea, however, not to give them material for mocking you. Keep records and show you are dedicated. The power of this example is very effective.

How then do you set about experimenting? As with any new method there is an element of novelty, and an initial period of free experimentation is a valuable learning experience.

Carefully following the instructions with the machine, make a series of exposures of any subject that comes to hand. Some people press-gang any passing person – friends, relatives, colleagues. Use this to become familiar with the machine and get the feel of the method. Make several photos of the same person over a period of time. Lay the prints out on the floor and see if you can spot differences. Invite others to join you. From this vast mass of data, your attention will be drawn, inevitably, to certain facets of the information.

It could be the fact that the thumb disappears after a yoga session, for example. Further define your field of enquiry and make more and more prints. You will then notice certain trends. Any discipline you have will increase your ability to make correlations. Don't forget – keep records. There's nothing worse than looking at a photograph with an outstanding feature and trying to remember if it was first or second in the series. Find our everything you can about the patient, any shock, trauma, domestic problem, past medical history, accident. Do not be shy about finding a sympathetic GP or researcher and discussing the results with them. In talking with them, new insights are often gained. They may become intrigued and offer themselves as volunteers or assistants.

The Kirlian phenomenon and its relation to pathology is still the subject of controversy. Psychological states, depending as they do on a number of interrelated states, are not directly measurable, though circumstantial evidence can be educed from the results some of the machines available today can produce. For example alterations in brain-waves can be evidence of brain malfunction though it will not tell us what sort of changes will necessarily occur.

The photographic result will depend in part on the disposition of the fingertips or the hands on the plate, the area of contact, the electrical parameters of the discharge, etc. Environmental factors such as air temperature, humidity and atmospheric pressure are said to play a modulating influence on the intensity of the corona discharges.

Not all approach a diagnostic situation with confidence. Victor Adamenko, one of the associates of Semyon Kirlian, noted with concern in 1988 the widely disparate types of equipment used to generate the fields which were bound to produce varying results. It is quite true that you have to find the type of machine that suits your way of working.

It is not the concern of this book to list the minutiae of differences between machines in use, since this would involve a great deal of technical information. Our aim is to describe and discuss the types of diagnosis and evaluation to which Kirlian photography can be most suitably applied, and the principles behind the production of the image itself.

However in the final analysis it is the reliability of the method under a wide variety of circumstances which is the validating factor. The writer introduced to the UK the idea of using the whole hand and the whole foot for psychological and medical diagnosis. The method has been used by scores of researchers in the UK and elsewhere in Europe. Thousands of photographs have been made, and used in day to day work in acupuncture, healing, counselling, meditation and diagnosis. In addition to the consensus amongst the practitioners, clients have agreed with the resulting assessments.

It is the opinion of all that by far the major factor is the part played by the balance of body energies or what Eastern philosophy would call the yin/yang balance of the body; the energy level, and the state of mental and psychological health. In other terminology – the integrity of the mind-body-spirit relationship is the major determinant of the shape and pattern of the image. This latter includes the functioning of the sympathetic and parasympathetic nervous system. So long as the hand or foot is carefully and consistently placed on the machine and the settings kept constant, a stream of useful information is obtained.

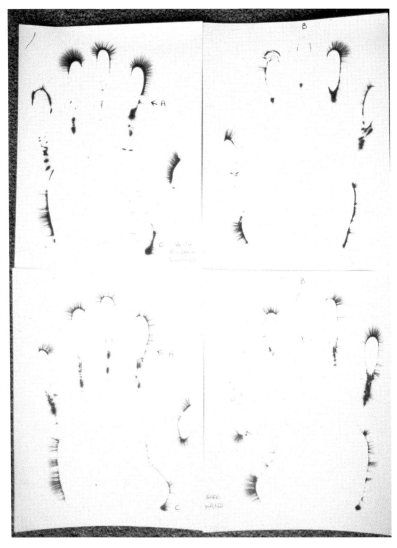

Experiment to determine the effect of moisture. Control gloved hand (top example) and same hand (bottom). Note that gaps and comparative strengths of corona are maintained.

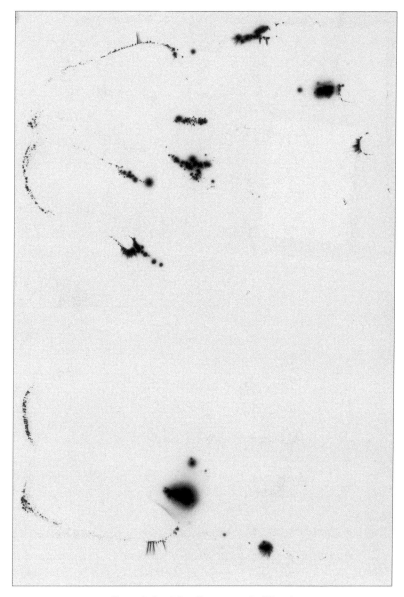

Example 1 – A 'totally overstretched' hand

*A woman in her 30s with a full-time job. Her husband had epilepsy; her mother has
had a nervous breakdown. She knows she must nourish herself.*
NOTE: *Note the lack of radiation, although the hands were carefully placed flat
on the camera.*

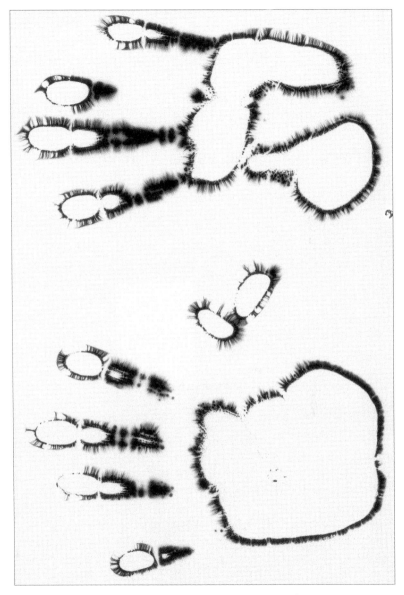

Example 2 – Subtle effects around the hand

Right hand of subject with subtle interference patterns round the fingertips.
Each finger's radiation has a different configuration and quality.
NOTE: *This is associated with sensitive people who are very aware of*
outside influences (fields).

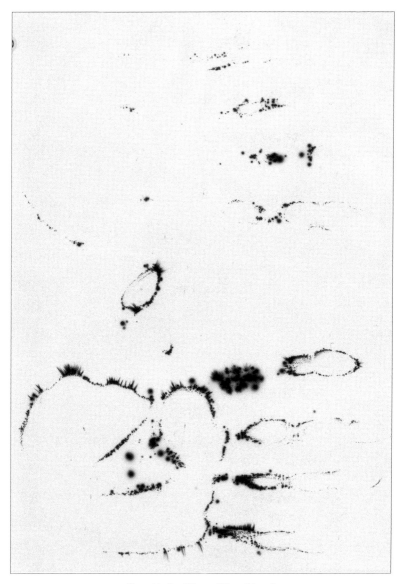

Example 3 – 'No confidence' hand

A man in his 20s – very shy – living reluctantly with his parents. Has difficulty expressing himself. The home environment difficult for his work as an artist.
NOTE: *'Colourless' appearance indicates lack of spontaneity and ability to relate. Subject needs counselling and support. The left hand (intuition and feeling) is even less radiant than the right hand (logic).*

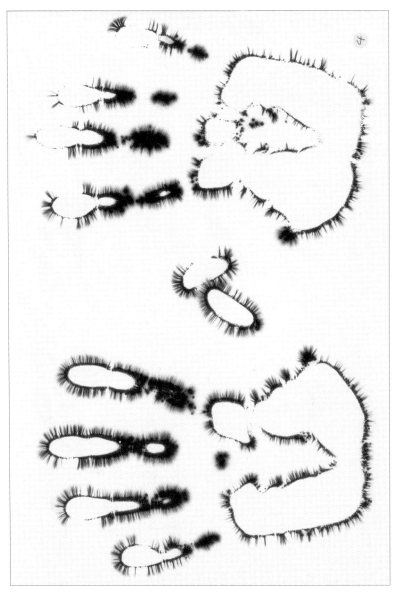

Example 4 – 'Under-utilized' hand

A man in his 30s recently made redundant from the computer industry. Well paid job but understretched. Polarity therapist. Knows he has a lot of discovering to do.
NOTE: *'Plenty of energy reservoirs (black areas down fingers). Left hand stronger than right hand. Also note inner band round fingertips which is a sign of strength of personality.*

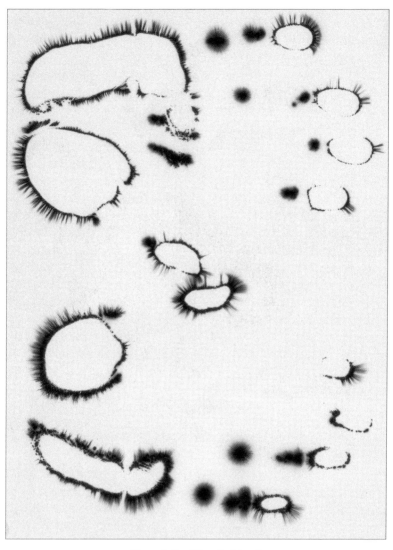

Example 5 – 'Changing' hand

*A woman in her 50s. She is reaching out spiritually and more comfortable
with her inner self.*
NOTE: *Presence of inner corona; radiations irregular and slightly disorientated but
never the less extant.*

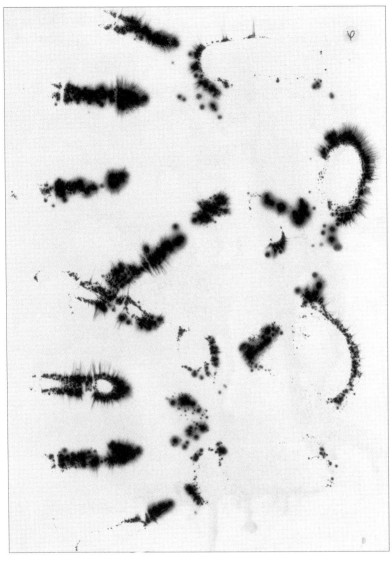

Example 6 – 'Recovering' hand

A man in his 20s recovering from exposure to drugs. He is trying to rebuild his self-confidence. Energy is blocked and he is currently unable to relate to others in a positive way.
NOTE: *Lack of any radiation in the fingertips. Irregularities at the base of the hands. Spheres of energy irregularly spaced throughout the hand.*

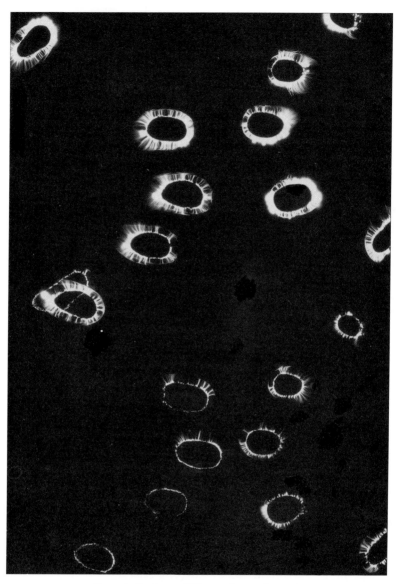

Example 7 – Compatibility test (reversed paper)

Left fingertip example shows the right hands of two friends photographed separately; the right example when their hands are placed on the apparatus at the same time.
NOTE: *Marked diminution in power of the corona and change in relative strength of the fingertips show incompatibility, a reduction in energy when the two radiation fields are in proximity.*

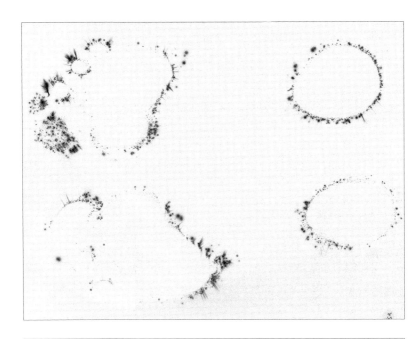

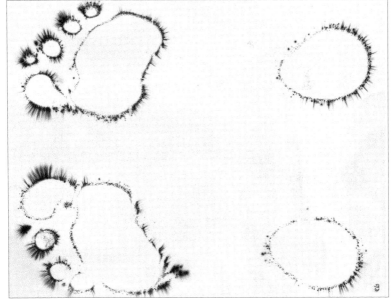

Example 8 – Feet – before and after spiritual healing

Note marked changes in the corona – more regularity and loss of blotches.

~4~

Kirlian photography in use

Casting my mind back to 1973 still provides me with the feeling of excitement as experiment after experiment showed me that I had stumbled on something of great value and significance. This chapter examines how the meanings of the patterns in the hands and feet were determined.

The original method was determined by a 'eureka' experience in 1973, the difference being that unlike Archimedes I was not in the bath at the time, but at my typewriter. As mentioned in the introduction, I had been aware of tingles in my hands for some years but could not interpret them and regarded the sensations as spurious and meaningless. It was after the first day of the first exhibition in Olympia and I knew I had to write something to inform people of the meaning of their prints. (No interpretation was offered on the stand on the first day). I was just making the photographs for the novelty value to the public in general.

I was wondering about the formative influences which made the irregularities in the Kirlian picture, as well as the cause of various lines and shapes which appeared in the palms of the hand. I realized that there might be a possible correlation between palmistry and Kirlian. As I thought this I received a shock along my fourth finger. I recall that at the time my hands were poised above the typewriter.

I thought instinctively about the main features of our daily life – spirituality (heart); creativity; work situation; leadership qualities; will power; relationships. As I thought of each, I received a shock in one of my fingers and in some cases down the length of the finger. The finger impression altered with each thought. Those intuitively conceived guidelines formed the basis of the diagnostic method in use today. I have found no reason to change or modify it, since it has served both me and the scores of Kirlian researchers in the UK well in the intervening period.

Not long afterwards, I noticed a correspondence between my finger shocks and the meanings of the fingers as in palmistry. For those who are new to this discipline, it is one of the most ancient occult sciences; it was commonly used in previous civilizations in the same way as astrology was used, at the Royal Courts. It's worth noting that Kepler, one of the world's foremost astronomers was a practising astrologer as well. During succeeding generations this discipline was more and more associated with fortune-telling and expediency. Its image today is still tarnished by this.

However there have been attempts for some decades to restore to palmistry its rightful heritage.

Beryl Hutchinson, author of the book *Your Life In Your Hands*, has made a special contribution in the field of detecting diseases and mineral imbalances in the body, through the information yielded by the patterns in the palm.

Dr. Charlotte Wolff, the British psychotherapist, comparing for example key lines in abnormal children with the same line in the hands of apes, considered that the hand is a visible part of the human brain.

Carl Gustav Jung, writing about palmistry, wrote that the findings and knowledge are of essential importance for psychologists, doctors and educationalists.

Palmistry has been found to be an excellent tool in preventive medicine as well as in psychotherapy.

The meanings of the areas of the hands according to my Kirlian method are as follows. The acupuncture and palmistry equivalents are indicated in the same section where applicable:

Left hand: the unconscious; your potential.

Palmistry: the unconscious, the past. The potential that the person is born with. The left hand is the 'receptive' hand, the 'being' side of a person's nature.

Right hand: Kirlian – the face you present to the world; how you translate ideas into practice. The conscious side.

Palmistry: indications show how the person is using their potential in the here and now, and shows the possibilities of future trends.

Left hand below base of little finger: (The right hand is a development of this as expressed in the social life.) Kirlian meaning – childhood memories; attitude to self.

Palmistry: moon. The unconscious, the dream life, ancestral memories. All the lunar qualities in a person. The moon is the symbol of the feminine principle.

Base of the thumb: sexual/emotional relationships. It is especially important to look at the balance between left and right hand. A strong radiation on the left hand, and a weak one on the right hand, indicates there is no response in the partner of the client. A strong radiation in the right and none in the left (much rarer) indicates that the person is not able to respond to what is offered.

Palmistry: Venus. Life energy, sexual-emotional energy. Libido. Love of harmony, beauty and sensuality.

Small finger: spiritual potential.

Palmistry: Mercury. The messenger of the ancient Greek Gods. Communication through speech and writing. Straightforwardness or deviousness of character can be seen. Sexual difficulties can also be traced.

Acupuncture: heart and small intestine.

Ring (fourth) finger: creativity, the psyche.

Palmistry: Apollo – The Sun God. Creativity, the ability to shine, success in the sense of creative work; love of the arts.

Acupuncture: triple warmer – endocrine system.

Middle finger: career/work situation.

Palmistry: Saturn – Teacher, wisdom, learning. Ability to take responsibility in life. Work and perseverance. Karma, fate.

Acupuncture: Pericardium – circulation meridian or vessel.

Index finger: Leadership potential and organizing ability.

Palmistry: Jupiter – expansion, ambition, of a worldly as well as a spiritual nature. Authority, ability to organize, self-assertive capability.

Acupuncture: large intestine.

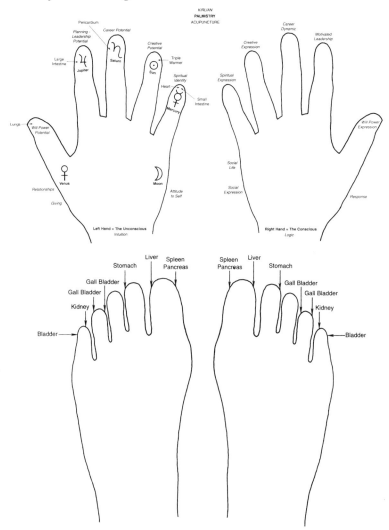

The significance of the hands and feet according to acupuncture, Kirlian and palmistry

The thumb: will power, practical matters.

Palmistry: Pluto. The tip: the first phalange is associated with will-power as it is related to the ego-structure and is most important in palmistry.

Acupuncture: lungs.

This was the basis of the making and giving of thousands of diagnoses at such events as the Mind/Body Festival in London and privately in the UK, Europe and the USA. Although arrived at intuitively and started with hesitancy, it has stood the test of time. When approaching this subject, always remember the basis of the Kirlian print, which is that the vital body of man, or the body of energy, should ideally fit like a glove over the physical body. How does this energy body fit with the physical body? Are there holes in the glove? If so, where and why? All holes and gaps are due to a mismatch between mind, body and spirit.

For the greatest perspective on the whole, the hands and feet should be photographed, preferably on the same occasion. It is the general body of opinion amongst the Kirlian researchers that the psyche is mainly reflected in the hands and the overall energy is represented in the feet.

Any differences between the left and right hand are important and are always significant. There is neurological evidence that the left brain is connected to the right side of the body, and the right brain is connected to the left side. The different workings of the brain (left brain is characterised as being logical, analytical, rational, sequential; the right brain is associated with intuitive, synthetic, holistic thinking) are well known to science. About the mechanism of the workings there is still controversy. About the only generally accepted fact is that the left hemisphere is specialized for language in more than 95% of right-handed people and 66% of left-handed people. Views about the function of the hemispheres are varied. Elkhonon Goldberg of the Albert Einstein College of Medicine, and Louis Costa of the University of Victoria think that the right hemisphere is the brain's jack-of-all-trades, a generalist that addresses new problems without preconceptions and tries many solutions until it hits on one that works. The left hemisphere, in contrast, is a specialist, solving familiar problems quickly and efficiently by using established methods.

In this theory they are supported by recently discovered anatomical differences between the hemispheres. The right hemisphere contains many long fibres that connect widely separated regions of the brain, each specialized for different aspects of information processing. This hemisphere can therefore mobilize a wide range of resources to attack a novel problem. The left hemisphere contains shorter fibres that provide rich interconnections within a given region to facilitate detailed processing of more well-defined tasks. It also contains larger volumes of 'associative cortex', the functions of which are thought to comprise the brain's most complex levels of information processing.

As another complementary classification of type, the notable scientist Paul MacLean divides the brain into three functions; the neomammalian or neocortical brain, the limbic brain and the reptile brain, which together comprise the triune brain. These types of function are common to the left and right brain. The reptile brain or the R-Complex is the oldest part, that concerned with aggression and territoriality; the limbic brain is concerned with feelings and emotions; the neomammalian or neocortical brain is described by MacLean as "the mother of invention and father of abstract thought".

In an integrated mind, all three brains work in harmony. Because the electrical activity of the brain is considerable, we would expect it to have considerable power to modify the electrical activity around the hand. It is therefore logical to examine the coherence of the patterns of the Kirlian picture which can give us valuable clues about which hemisphere is predominant.

Thus a picture with a weak left hand and a strong right hand will indicate a person who is out of touch with their own subconscious mind and might act in such a way that is not true to type. A strong left hand and weak right hand indicates that the person is in touch with their own true nature but they have difficulty in translating these ideals and ideas in practical terms.

Aspiring researchers please take note that however spectacular the information gleaned from any method is, we should never make dogmatic statements. Information itself should only be one source of our output to the client. We cannot be completely certain that stimulus A causes result B, and jumping to conclusions may adversely affect a process of self-learning. On the other hand, if we suspend all judgement until we have cast iron proof (or in statistical terms a

100% correlation), we may risk waiting a very long time and miss out on a valuable aid to our diagnosis.

We are looking for a balance of probabilities that the two are interconnected.

To summarize on the dynamics of the use of Kirlian: it is always useful to have more than one method to assist in an overall appreciation of the individual. The following dynamics are involved:

1.   The practitioner's sight of the Kirlian photograph and the information derived from it.

2.   The client seems to know what the photograph means and we have often had the remark, 'I thought it was going to be like that'. It is useful for the client to see for him or herself the changes to the balance of the energy field during the therapist's work.

3.   Information derived from the field of the individual, which is fed into the nervous system of the practitioner. This happens far more frequently than is imagined and is the basis for the 'gut reaction' that most of us rely on.

4.   Application of the knowledge and experience of the practitioner, including the ability to draw out the perceived facts from the client.

What is the most useful method of going about our work with the Kirlian apparatus? What are the common rules towards approaching the whole method of using any aid in a method of assessment? This analogy may help.

A number of you no doubt tend your garden. I certainly do. How do we set about our task? First, we look at the overall picture. What is the general appearance of the garden? What is the condition of the flowerbeds, the trees and the lawn?

When we have taken the overview, we look in closer detail. Does the lawn need cutting? Is fertilizer required? Do we need to weed the beds? Then we think ahead. Do we want flowers to bloom all through the year? If so, what plans should we make for planting and sowing. Only a very unwise person would close their eyes, walk over to a flowerbed, and throw seeds around just hoping that they would grow somehow. And yet, many people take just the same attitude with trying to help friends. Practitioners fall into the same trap. The reported problem (professionals call it the presenting problem) is seldom the cause. For example I might have a headache. This is in fact due to having rows with my wife. I have rows with my wife because I am jealous of someone with whom she may be having an affair. I am jealous because I am insecure. I am insecure because I cannot find the courage to have a talk with her. This is because my own mother was dominating and she never listened to me. See how one symptom – the headache – is at the end of a long chain of cause and effect. In jargon terms, therefore, look at the macro before the micro.

The help that we can give anyone will only start the process of healing and regeneration. We human beings are a paradox. On the one hand we are on the look-out for any novelty, or what Eric Fromm called in his excellent book *The Fear of Freedom* the *Magic Helper*. On the other hand when the instruments of change are presented to us we think of all sorts of reason, why we should not pursue them. 'O Lord, make me pure, but not yet' was the cry of St. Augustine, the great theologian!

Nevertheless, instant cures do not exist. As such I view with deep suspicion the activities of certain evangelist/healers – notably those from the USA. They whip people into a fever of enthusiasm and often use their inherent suggestibility to temporarily cancel out physical symptoms. Studies by doctors have found very little evidence that healing occurs on anything other than a temporary basis.

There are two elements to every act of helping. What flows through you and what flows out of your mouth. Of the two I regard the former as more important. In very great summary, and using Kirlian photography as an example, the diagnostic opinion and subsequent help has a number of roots: the information given by the print; information volunteered by the client; the experience of the practitioner in previous cases; their training with regard to the many and varied conditions of the human being; the time and energy that both client and practitioner are prepared to spend working through the process of change; last but not least the intuition of the practitioner, which is the sum total of his or her whole being.

Bearing this in mind the practitioner may adopt the following procedure. After the photo has been made, show it to the client. Much information is given subliminally. You may ask them what they feel about the photo. In a surprising number of cases, the client will respond by saying 'I thought it would be like that'. Try to get them involved as much as possible. Identify the main feature which will probably be the difference between the left and right hand, or one finger and another, encourage them to talk about that aspect of their personality as it relates to that finger according to the charts in this book. Analyse the inner corona (yin or feminine energy) distinctly from the radiations (yang or male energy). A firm and continuous inner corona is a sign of strength and integrity; the radiations indicate flare and initiative.

One symptom can have many causes. As a general guide, the less you say, the better. Let the client draw their own conclusions, for example – my energy is low because......, my creativity is lacking because... ...; my intuition is weak because I .... Skilful leading questions are of far more therapeutic value than 'telling' a person about their condition, though inspiration as a stimulus must be given its rightful place. On the holistic level, the Kirlian picture can be seen as a catalyst, a stimulus, an indication of the starting point for a discussion during which self-understanding will be enhanced.

Each experience will teach you more about the method. Correlations will build up in your mind. All the information will be filed away in your memory. With clarity of focus and address the intuition will be honed and developed. With careful recording and working without other practitioners and combining disciplines, a very useful framework of knowledge will slowly but surely build up. Research should be a continuous process. Have an ever-watchful eye for an interesting picture. Don't let it 'escape'. Ask if you can make a photocopy and send it to the client.

My overall view of the whole question of helping others along the path of enlightenment is this. I believe that everyone has the image of the highest quality of attainment and behaviour within them to which they can aspire if they wish.

I have always been struck by the works of Plato and Socrates who I believe were the fathers of many of our present-day tenets of law, psychology and sociology. I was particularly struck by Socrates' successful attempt to draw out of one of the slaves of Menon, who had never studied geometry, the proposition about the square of the hypotenuse. We all have all knowledge within us. The vast majority of people who come to me as clients know what the solution to their problem is by their own admission. Time and time again I hear the words 'I knew that but I needed someone to confirm it'. The skill is in drawing it out, perhaps functioning as a mirror. This is where the diversity of all our skills and abilities can be put to best use.

~5~

Navigating the Minefield

What causes things to happen? To understand our universe we must postulate a separate entity called 'mind' or 'spirit' or 'soul'. These may be manifestations of religious bigotry or the cries in the wilderness of the enlightened ones.

There are two distinct groups of opinion about the nature of the human mind or consciousness. One viewpoint – let's call it the metaphysical viewpoint – holds that the human mind is of a non-material, spiritual or even semi-divine and mystical character, akin to the soul. This mind resides in the material human body without actually becoming a part of it.

Another philosophy, the 'mechanistic' stand-point, includes the assumption that the universe is primarily physical and made up of large 'hunks' of matter. Its actions and attributes can be explained by the laws of mechanics. Future performance can be calculated from past behaviour patterns. It is predictable and exact. The whole mechanism is determined by its parts and there is no intrinsic wholeness separate from the sum of the parts. The mind, therefore, is composed of the same kind of stuff that makes up the physical universe. It is materially based in character, and it is probably connected with the function of the brain and the central nervous system.

Proponents of the metaphysical viewpoint would include phenomena which are not predictable, stable or causal. They would not invalidate a phenomenon because it cannot be understood or explained in terms of the known laws of physics. They accept that any phenomena are a totality of known and unknown laws.

An approach trying to bring the two views together has the difficult task of aggregating these two world views. How do molecular structures react together to produce awareness? How do electro-magnetic fields integrate? What are their natures and their characteristics? Is the mind separate from the brain? Do two or more sets of parameters impinge on or complement each other? Why does it matter at all if we understand what is going on?

The majority of scientists in the Western World see the two starting points as mutually exclusive, though more and more are moving over to the view of Sir James Jeans that "the universe begins to look more like a great thought than a great machine". Currently, Western science is slow to gear to or to prepare to deal with these mental or spiritual forces. Investigative programmes on TV, whilst leaving the door open to the possibility of a reality beyond the physical, often take as their basic hypothesis the possibility of fraud or, at the least, bad scientific method on the part of the practitioner, or suggestibility on the part of the client, for the apparent reality of phenomena under discussion. More commonly, papers written by those with the metaphysical approach are rejected or ignored.

At this point we might take a historical look at the extent of prejudice that any proponent of new thinking – or shall we say visionary thinker – has to suffer. Here are two examples of the treatment of innovators by the press.

From an American newspaper of less than 100 years ago:

> "A man was arrested yesterday, charged with attempting to obtain money under false pretences. He claimed he was promoting a device whereby one person could talk to another several miles away, by means of a small apparatus and some wire. Without doubt this man is a fraud and an unscrupulous trickster and must be taught that the American public is too smart to be the victim of this and similar schemes. Even if this insane idea worked it would have no practical value other than for circus side shows."

The man arrested was Alexander Graham Bell and his 'small apparatus and some wire' was the first telephone, a device that within a few years would revolutionize the very concept of communications.

Nikola Tesla, the American inventor, lived in seclusion most of his life but he liked to receive a normally incredulous press on each

January 8th, his birthday, and had the habit of announcing a new invention over coffee and cake.

In 1926, to the vast amusement of the press, he had predicted the coming of television, when

> *"we shall be able to witness the inauguration of a President or the playing of a world series baseball game, just as though we were there."*

The press described him as a dreamer, who imagined that

> *"people will be able to see distant events like the sorceress or the magic crystal of fairy tales and legends."*

I am reminded of the wry statement by Dr. Kettering, the great inventoy, who is said to have commented:

> *"People are all in favour of new ideas, provided they are exactly like the old ones."*

The above examples relate to claims which, although appearing far-fetched in their time, related to mechanical instruments and apparatus. How much greater, then, can we expect the prejudice to be when relating to non-physical matters, such as auras and the like. Traditionally there has been an antipathy between scientists and mystics. Many scientists close their mind to the whole topic of telepathy, clairvoyance, pre-cognition and more or less the whole range of psychic phenomena. This in spite of well documented evidence for, for example, distant perception and the wealth of circumstantial evidence about the connectedness of energy fields.

What attitude do we take towards the difficult problem of understanding Kirlian photography? Does it matter if we understand it so long as it works? Towards Kirlian photography and other disciplines which depend on a wider appreciation of consciousness, there are a number of commonly held points of view:

Cynical

If I cannot see it, feel it, touch it, smell it, hear it, then it does not exist. Such so-called phenomena are second class phenomena, inferior to science, fit for the gullible and lonely psychology.

Atheistic
The so-called 'Kirlian' effect is due purely to artefacts, i.e. interaction between the film or paper, the object, and the electrical field produced by the device. Anyone with sufficient grasp of science and physiology who has studied the development of high-voltage corona discharge photography can explain the phenomenon. Any so called 'diagnostic' value is only due to the intuition of the therapist or interpreter.

Pragmatic/materialist
There is sufficient evidence that Kirlian can monitor physical parameters such as the activity of sweat glands, skin resistance, pressure, temperature, etc. If it can be demonstrated that these parameters reflect changes in the physiological and psychological states of the subject then the method may have diagnostic value.

Parapsychological
Although 'physical' parameters such as sweat may play a part in producing the corona effect, these conventional parameters are not the only cause of the image. The phenomena can only be fully understood if the existence of an energy surround, 'aura', or 'bioplasmic body' is accepted, although their dynamics may not be fully understood by conventional science. This is not sufficient reason for their rejection as a working hypothesis.

Enthusiastic
Physical parameters such as sweat are not relevant to the information given by the Kirlian photo, which reveals for the first time the product of the interaction between the soul and physical factors. The colours and shapes are revealing for the first time what mystics and clairvoyants have been seeing for centuries.

The above is a broad range of the types of attitude both on the part of the public and of some scientists to any para... phenomenon. The word para – 'beside', 'beyond', 'irregular' – comes from the Greek and is used descriptively or pejoratively. Any extreme view tends to preclude a willingness to countenance the opposite position so juxtaposition of such stances tend to be unproductive.

    The use of high-frequency, high-voltage electric fields to stimulate light emissions, mainly applied to humans, has been christened

Kirlian Photography. It differs from other induced luminescence techniques in that a corona discharge is formed. In addition it does not use photomultiplier tubes to detect the emitted light, but rather uses a variety of light-sensitive surfaces including photographic film, paper, video, fluorescent screens or electrostatic surfaces.

It would be good to remind ourselves of Ockham's Razor – from William of Ockham or Occam (c.1300–c.1349) – which is that the best theory to explain any phenomenon is the simplest theory that accounts for the various aspects of it; i.e. that it shaves off all unnecessary assumptions. It is strategically important because both ends of the spectrum tend to devise elaborate structures of guesswork to account for what they see, or don't see. The materialists' tunnel view obliges them to rule out non-physical explanations as impossible.

The human being represents the ultimate paradox; an essence which many consider to be eternal and immortal in an envelope – the human body – which is contained within the framework of time and space. We are faced with the impossible task of observing ourselves. The 'us' that looks though our eyes is the 'us' that is partly aware that we possess observational facilities but are not bound by them. Everyone, because of the way they are constructed, has an irreducible facility to see the world in a spatial way, ably assisted by our five senses of hearing, smell, touch, tasting and seeing. This has been installed in us owing to the necessity of a built-in perception mechanism, including the flight or fight response, to afford us the means of physical protection. This was required in primordial times. Things are or appear to be 'a long way away'. Objects are 'large' or 'small' or moving fast or slow. Touch is gentle or rough. We have been given this perceptual facility primarily for our own physical protection.

However, parapsychology and paraphysics are starting to show mankind – particularly cynical Western man – that we have other built-in facilities for perceiving the world of sensation which interpenetrates and interposes on the hitherto measurable world mentioned above. These two comprise the meeting point that enables us to construct a semantic universe using ideas and images from the non-physical as well as the physical world. The two facilities in combination provide a stage for an exploration of the paradox that man is both body and spirit. Present existential structures are a product and a combination of these two roots and arguably provide the only inte-

grated functioning system for mankind to fully understand the implications of his own nature.

As we have seen, the boundary between the mental and physical
universe has been proved to be unclear and ill-defined as has the division between the animate and inanimate. To what extent are objects
imbued with consciousness? How are we to treat the field effects of
the discoveries of radionics and of Harold Saxton Burr? Given sufficiently sensitive scientific instruments, should the field attributes of
an object – animate or inanimate – be regarded as a legitimate part of
that object, albeit more subtle? The idea that 'nothing' separates
objects in the physical world is shown to be redundant, but this is lost
on the societally programmed psychically oriented mind-set of the
majority of the population. True, the idea of a God transcends this
model, but God is seen as a metaphysical being living in eternity to
which the known laws of the universe are not applicable.

Amidst this, the phenomenon of Kirlian photography has to be
fitted in somehow. Is it a purely physical phenomenon; an artefact of
the bombardment of objects by high-energy particles, or is it evidence
– circumstantial or otherwise – of the juxtaposition of a non-physical
universe on the physical plane?

At this point it might be interesting to see how a professional person views Kirlian as a discipline which might have a practical application. Let's look at the view expressed at the 1990 International
Kirlian conference by a consultant psychiatrist Dr. Peter Haslam. He
is aware of some of the potentialities of the Kirlian method, having
been introduced to it in the first wave of enthusiasm in the 1970s. He
has a private clinic in Harrogate, Yorkshire, England. He comments
about his work with colleagues:

"Professor Peter Venables who is Professor of Psychology at the
University of York had been researching into people with a schizophrenic problem. He developed a series of tests which related to skin
characteristics. He was measuring skin conduction recovery time. He
passed a current and observed the pattern it makes on an elec-
tromyographic device, and found that patients suffering from schizophrenic illness produced a particular pattern of skin conduction
recovery time which was different to a normal control population.

"One of the theories to do with psychiatric illness is that it relates
to changes in monoamine metabolism, i.e. the chemical transmitter
agents in the brain, which relate to changes in mood, behaviour, etc.

Changes in certain of these monoamines, in particular noradrenaline, occur in the nerves and in the nerve–muscle junctions and probably therefore in the skin. It may be that changes in adrenaline or other monoamines such as serotonin might be producing changes in skin recovery time. This would explain changes in anxiety at a chemical level and changes seen in tome types of depressive illness. Such a non-invasive method as Kirlian photography might be able to show up such changes in a different way.

"For a method to be useful in a medical practice in general and in a psychiatric practice in particular, the photographing of these emanations needs to be done simply and readily without the need to control too vigorously all the possible variables which researchers may care to investigate. The diagnosis and prognosis need to be affected in an out-patient clinic without worrying too much about the exact temperature of the room or the strength of the developer or fixer. A reasonably standardized procedure must be able to be followed by a variety of clinicians and therapists with some level of test-retest reliability both in the way in which the test is operated and in the interpretation of the results. If variations in the external environment too readily alter the picture produced, then it is unlikely to be greatly useful as a diagnostic and clinical tool for the average practising therapist.

"Some enthusiastic users who are practised in the technique may be able to interpret the progress of an individual or the problem because of their own particular expertise and experience derived over a long period of time.

"The internal environment of the client will vary from day to day, and for a test to be reliable at diagnosing something, there must be some discernible factor which overrides these more immediate changes in mood and circumstance which the patient may experience from hour to hour. If smoking a cigarette or drinking coffee will change the picture in that it will blue the clarity of the underlying picture, this technique will be very difficult to use in everyday psychiatric out-patients, because you cannot control these things in patients.

"In our experimental series, we took handprints of supposedly normal subjects. What is normal? We did not try to correlate with acupuncture. We looked at age and sex (and in the case of female subjects, stages in menstrual cycle), plus records of any medication and any products that might affect the central nervous system, e.g. alcohol, cigarettes. If such products were taken within the normal range for

the population, then it would not be helpful if these changes inter-
fered too much with the Kirlian print. If they were excessive, then it
would be useful to be able to pick them up.

"Using normal photographic paper, pictures were taken. Another
problem was that some types of depressed patients may become
somewhat suspicious or paranoid about what we are doing. Patients
with manic illness may be too restless to concentrate long enough to
keep their hand on the machine whilst the exposure is being made.
Stress, anxiety and tension shows as a trend and the changes one
would get in the skin and other tissues are to do with that increased
stress. Some of the prints are extremely abnormal and are an indication of the potential suitability of the method for assisting in the diagnostic process."

What is the opinion of an acupuncturist? Dr. J. M. Tung, also
speaking at the International Kirlian Conference in 1990, uses it in
his daily work. He comments:

> *"If we want to have a holistic understanding of human
> nature, to see only the organs and the anatomical physio-
> logical system is too restrictive. Acupuncture, before being
> a medicine, is knowledge of life in the Taoist tradition."*

He believes that the information of the corona, and of the bio-
luminescence, are better separated. With acupuncture it is not the
organs themselves that are linked to the various fingers and toes; it is
rather their function. For example with the liver. In acupuncture the
liver meridian is connection with the hormonal system, blood circulation, etc. You can have a healthy physical organ and have a gynae-
cological problem at the same time.

The corona represents the yin energy; the electro-biological bio-
luminescence represents the yang energy. The ratio of 1:3 in extent is
healthy, coupled with regularity.

The function of the Kirlian photography and acupuncture is five-
fold.

1.   It is an energetic identity card with a knowledge of the
quantity, quality and the dynamic of the energy.
2.   It is an energy diagnosis including, where appropriate, a
clinical diagnosis.

3.   It provides a means of checking a therapy. If acupuncture is helpful to interpret Kirlian photography every intervention can be monitored.

4.   If we compare the evolution between successive photos we get a prognosis of the illness.

5.   Kirlian photography allows early warning and prevention if we know that a perturbation of the electro-luminescence can appear before the clinical symptoms. For example myocardial infarction can show on the Kirlian print between three weeks and 24 hours before an electrocardiogram at the clinic gives any indication.

The very subject matter itself is a challenge for even the most open-minded of scientists since so many types of cause have to be considered. Even Dr. Ion Dumitrescu himself, a respected and knowledgeable researcher, may have been lulled by reductionist thinking. He says in his book *Electrographic Methods in Medicine and Biology*: "The phenomenon of electroluminescence in gases is the principal mechanism for the production of the image in Kirlian Photography. Electrical non-homogeneities on the surface, or in the vicinity, of the object exposed in the field generated by the power source are transposed into images by luminescent discharges in ionized gases, due to the very high applied potential."

There are similarities between the emanations of the Kirlian image and holographs. The principle of holography is that a small sample of the whole contains an image of the whole organism. Coherent waves may be being given out by the human body, or a plant, and these may impinge on the physical body. The electrical processes within the body are very highly organized and the interaction between them and the electrical excitation of the Kirlian apparatus is the cause of the visible patterns. When a Kirlian photo is made, the pictures are then examined visually or subjected to quantification by densitometric analysis.

As implied above, the electrography is an instantaneous record of continuous biological activity but which does not represent the morphological structure.

What happens during a Kirlian exposure? There is an interference with the electromagnetic or ionic field of the object generated by the acceleration of the charged particles. The resulting interference patterns produce the distinctive pictures on the photosensitive material.

The 'cold' emission of electrons results in photon ionization and the consequent liberation of photon particles.

These are modified by the internal energy field of force in which the entire body resonates and does so for as long as it lives. Dr. R. Bathula, an Indian researcher, notes that in order to produce similar fluctuations in patterns in non-living material the electrical parameters – that is the voltages – at the electrode plate have to be varied by the order of thousands of volts. The body itself only shows changes in the millivolt range. This lends weight to the idea that the whole living body resonates with auric energy – which Eastern philosophy would call 'prana'.

The electromagnetic field caused by the accelerator throws the electrons at the interface into an oscillation. When one of the electrons hits the neighbouring electrons, energy is released in quantum packets called photons. This is because the kinetic energy of the particle is affected due to the collision and consequent loss of energy. Photons are fundamental particles of light. This is why the image takes the form of light.

The number of electrons that are released is dependent on the auric field intensity and its resonance, which also determines the basic energy level of the electron before it is set into an oscillation, by defining the number of photons released, and also the image formed. Thus, the phenomenon of photon emission, plus the different wavelengths of the visible light spectrum and invisible radiation such as ultraviolet and infrared, is the essence of the photograph. Photographic paper is not sensitive to infrared light. That is why a red light can be used with impunity when making black and white exposures. The stimulus of the charged particles cause an emission of light, and this contains elements of ultraviolet light. This may comprise the inner corona which we see in the photograph, though no definitive assessments have yet been made.

Each disease produces a typical characteristic difference in fields. In anxiety neurosis the fingertips do not show at all; in hypertension there is a distinct area which is depicted more brightly than the other areas. Different stages in malignancy of cancer patients show different patterns.

Bioelectrography has been found to cover such diverse fields as medicine, yoga, and spiritualism. Allopathy apart, distinct patterns have been found in the case of homoeopathic pills. In the chanting of yoga, a tremendous change has been observed 'before' and 'after'. The Kirlian pictures reflect the changes in entropy of a living system.

What is the relationship if any between the Kirlian photograph and the aura that mystics and clairvoyants see around the human body? Kirlian photography is in essence a record of interference patterns. It's a stress graph; not the whole apple but a slice, not the three-dimensional coloured surround that mystics see shimmering around the body. The full aura is far more subtle in its intrinsic nature than any reflection or aspect of the surround revealed by the Kirlian method. Disturbances seen in the aura are related to changes in the Kirlian photo or acupuncture meridians or voltage gradients and these are the nearest we have come so far to recording the detailed aura photographically.

In human beings, the problems presented are more complex still. Electro-magnetic field patterns round the body are affected both by the psychology and the physiology of the subject, whereas in plants, health and disease are mainly reflected. However there is one methodological problem which must stand as a background to all research.

In 1988, Victor Adamenko said:

"The scientific community has yet to accept high frequency photography as a totally reliable tool because of two factors. The first is high-frequency photography's enthusiastic use and interpretation by practitioners who have failed to apply rigorous scientific methods to their work. The second cause for concern has been the widely disparate types of equipment used to create the images, which are bound to produce varying results."

The lack of standardization is noticed by many researchers, such as Cope (1980); Ebraham and Williams (1982). Hubacher and Moss, prominent researchers from the USA, stated as early as 1979:

"It is important to stress that we are currently exploring several different 'Kirlian' instruments and that each has characteristics unique to itself."

From a technical point of view it is difficult to modulate accurately very high voltage current (up to 30 kV) over a wide spectrum of frequencies and wave forms without incurring great expense. The lack of funding has caused researchers to build typically simple circuits and the introduction of more versatile equipment is needed internationally.

Media coverage of the 1980s not only reflects curiosity but cynicism. Gillie, 1986, claimed that "a photograph of the human aura provides the perfect pretext to talk about anything".

As we have seen above, battles to have something accepted are 'par for the course'. Consider the affront to the Roman Catholic Church when Copernicus presumed to question the authority of its teaching with regard to the solar system. He was pilloried at the time but now the hypothesis is accepted. When the community accepts something it merely means that it stands until disproved.

In other fields, the existence of forces is determined by inference: for example the existence of ephemeral elements high up in the periodic table that are so unstable they are said to exist for only a few thousandths of a second.

Other determinations of reality are made anecdotally, experimentally and circumstantially. For example few would doubt the existence of love, yet this factor can neither be measured or proved. We believe it because we see its effect on individuals. We 'know' that it is true. No scientist would dream of suggesting that love does not exist because he or she does not have instruments that are capable of measuring its nature and extent. I have of course taken an extreme example to make a point.

In the case of Kirlian photography, what level and method of proof is required for Kirlian phenomena to be accepted? Do we wait for the definitive proof, controlling all variables?

In general terms, the demonstration of a safe and satisfactory correlation between the size and shape of a corona discharge and the mental, psychological and physical condition of the subject is necessary. Discipline must be applied to the choice of machine, the setting of the controls and the duration and nature of the wave form. The big advantage for the Kirlian researcher is that the variations in the type of photo are so marked that correlations can be made between the patterns and the results of studies by other methods, e.g. psychiatry, acupuncture, reflexology.

Kirlian can be seen as a bridge between the visible and invisible worlds, between physics and paraphysics, between psychology and parapsychology. For an adequate understanding of the dynamics involved it is necessary to adopt a multi-disciplinary approach.

Let us return for a moment to my experiments listed above following on Harold Saxton Burr's work on energy fields.

One of the taken-for-granted situations is the mechanism whereby the body assumed a certain shape. What tells the body to grow – but also to stop growing – at a particular point in time? The human body in general, and cells in particular, are remarkably complex constructions. Cells contain DNA, and have the ability to work in harmony with groups of other cells to create organs, blood, bones, muscle tissue, etc. Each cell has an electric potential. Although the cell membrane is a mere 200 nanometres across, it generates 50–60 millivolts. This translates up to approximately ten million volts per metre. In addition to this electric field is an electromagnetic field – the conglomerate effect of cells acting in groups. The body can therefore be seen as a product of an immense beehive of interrelating fields of incredibly complex shape which give instructions about the growth and development of the human body. The patterns are determined by the DNA of the person. DNA holds records of all physiological information about the subject, with the scope to hold data about a person's psychological well-being. We inherit our mother's and father's DNA which not only contains formative information about our physical make-up but our personality characteristics. There is an interplay between the power of the DNA of the parents and that of the child. These formative influences can be referred to as a 'morphogenetic field'. In common parlance the word 'aura' can be substituted. This is our being, a surface field which emanates into space.

Is the idea of 'soul' redundant? Soul in this context I define as the equivalent of our unique way of thinking and being. Man is distinguished from most of the animal kingdom because of his/her ability to perform acts of altruism, to sacrifice for others' benefit. We are able to become irrational. The fact that we can have a sense of self, i.e. a discrete consciousness, indicates that there is more to us than a mechanical computerized thinking process. Machines and computers have no awareness. Each person has a unique 'print' and this is influenced by their nervous, emotional or thinking state. The soul itself cannot be photographed. It is the integrity between the soul (basic nature), the body (physical structure) and the mind (free will, thought) that is the remit of Kirlian.

When a photographed object is placed on the film or paper and charge applied, free electrons from the electrode excite electrons in biological and non-biological environmental molecules, gradually creating an avalanche effect which will eventually lead to the formation of a corona discharge as the electrons and ions recombine. As a result, several types of electromagnetic and non-electromagnetic radiation are emitted including radio waves, ultraviolet and visible light, X-rays, thermal energy and acoustic waves. The resulting electrons and photons generated by these complicated processes are traditionally measured using photo-sensitive material, e.g. film. Since the gas molecules surrounding the sample also contribute to the corona discharge, it has been estimated that as much as 85% of the total emissions are non-biological in origin. However, when hands are photographed, a certain proportion of these environmental molecules will be of biological origin, being secreted through pores of the skin.

The micro-environment surrounding the skin consists of water molecules, electrolytes (e.g. sodium ions), ammonia and urea. If filters are incorporated to screen out non-biological components of the signal and spectroscopes are used to determine the frequency of the emitted light, (as in the case of spontaneous emissions), ultraviolet is found to be the predominant frequency. In addition to measuring the chemical secretions of the body in the micro-environment, corona discharge photography is influenced by the electromagnetic properties of the skin and underlying tissues. It is therefore a truly holistic technique in that it measures several biological properties simultaneously.

All living bodies are surrounded by an electric field. The Kirlian apparatus excites the electrons of the cells associated with the skin. The excitation and the discharge produces photons – particles of light, a quantum of electromagnetic radiation. These are the stages of energy exchange when a photo is taken. At first, the molecules are at rest round the body. When the apparatus is switched on, energy is infused on to the body, resulting in a change of energy state of the electrons on the surface. The change in momentum results in light particles or photons being released. The orderliness or symmetry of the release patterns determines the nature of the picture. High-energy particles are ultraviolet light; lower energy ones are infrared.

It is necessary to adjust the machine to a standard level so as not to disturb all the molecules, otherwise blandness and overcharge will be the result. The art is to set the machine to provide just enough stimulus to 'test' the corona, and examine the nature and complexity of the discharges.

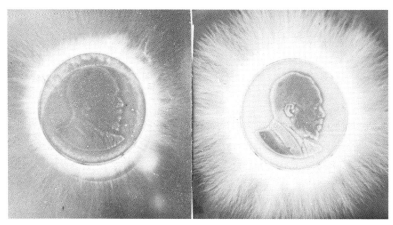

A coin before and after being touched by a healer.
Note brighter glow.

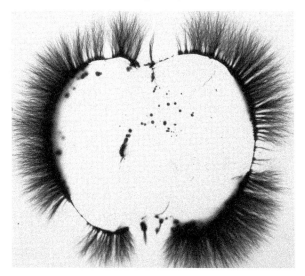

An apple cut in half. The gaps in the corona were not
understood until a few days later when the relevant areas were
seen to be bruised.

The Kirlian electro-photograph shows how the physical outline of the object corresponds to the reflected pattern of the life energy of the object. The Kirlian field is a product of all nervous activity formed by states of mind and body which affects the state of tension of the nervous system. Living structures, particularly the structure of human beings, are in fact arrangements of atoms and molecules held together by forces creating a biomagnetic field. In general, inanimate objects with no free will of their own, e.g. coins, only have the ability to re-radiate an imprinted field such as that imprinted by a healer. Living objects such as the hand are in a state of flux.

Why are there pictures that do not appear to have aura? Every living thing radiates a field of some sort otherwise it would die. Fields, and the necessary electrical activity in the brain, are vital for the support of life. There are two reasons why the Kirlian picture should not show. First, the emitted field may be very weak, and may not prevent the static charge going to ground. Secondly, the frequency of the emitted field may be different from that given out by the Kirlian apparatus. In this case, a variable frequency generator will be the most valuable tool in probing the changes that occur in disease states, both mental and physical.

Living things can be visualized as being enveloped in a sea of electromagnetic energy of various types. Sometimes the sea is calm. When disease has struck then it is turbulent. In Kirlian photography lies the possibility of monitoring this seascape. Kirlian primarily records the waves or high points. Ideally the human field – representing a balance between the mind, body and spirit – will be stable. However in the real world imbalance is the rule rather than the exception. The nature of these imbalances and their extent shows us the probable source of the problem.

According to Inyushin, Kirlian images are caused by a 'bioplasma', a stream of subatomic particles that move in and out of living tissue, and this bioplasma could give important information about the life process – including pathological changes. Experimental evidence collected during the late 1970s suggested that all objects, and especially living objects, contain and are surrounded by diffuse clouds of matter-energy probably best considered as a superconductive plasma state.

However, experimental evidence presented for the existence of biological plasma (bioplasma), from the areas of Kirlian photography, acupuncture and studies of biological fields, are largely explainable in conventional terms without invoking the existence of biological plasma, according to researcher Quickenden. Oldfield agrees: "Whilst we recognise the validity of the phenomena he found, we do not think there is any reason to invent a new kind of field force to account for it, when existing physical laws can explain what is happening."

Adamenko, sees the photographs as demonstrating 'cold emission of electrons', and American scientists have substituted the term 'cold emission of electrons' with the more familiar term, 'corona discharge'. Corona discharge is the light emitted by an electrode when a high-voltage electric field is applied to the electrode. In the case of corona-discharge photography, the object being photographed (in our case the human body) is acting as an electrode. When the subject is placed onto the film, an electrical interaction occurs which causes photon emission to affect the film. The image captured on the film reflects the dynamic relationship between the externally generated electric field and the energy emitted from the subject.

Pehak suggested in 1976 that most of the variations in the images of the corona can be accounted for by the presence of moisture on or within the subject's surface. This response may be useful in the detection and quantification of moisture in the subject, through the orderly modulation of the image due to the various levels of moisture therein. However it has been shown by Elklit in 1990 that variations in humidity from 40% to 70% have no measurable influence on the images, and the insertion of a polyethylene sheet, an effective sweat/moisture barrier between the finger and the film, has no effect on a corona.

Victor Adamenko, who was a colleague of Semyon Kirlian, queried the make-up of the emissions. He was able to exclude the role of visible light, by showing that an image could still be obtained on a luminescent screen which was not sensitive to light. No doubt the light (together with ultraviolet and X-rays) contribute a share, but he showed that something else was responsible for the main part of the image. This 'something else' was likely to be either ions or electrons. He therefore interposed a very thin aluminium sheet between the object and the luminescent screen. The image was as good as ever, even though the aluminium was opaque to ions. He concluded that the picture was 'drawn' by means of electrons. In a later experiment the stream of electrons was directed via a vacuum to a screen. It was discovered that the image could be deflected by a magnet in exactly the same way as one can deflect the image on a TV screen and thus proved that it was made by electrons.

Writers of the esoteric say that Kirlian photography can reveal a subject's character, emotional state, astral body, the energy field, the doppleganger or even his very soul. However, many scientists are not convinced. Professor Ellison suggests that there is very little about the process that is strictly paranormal. Julian Kenyon's views on Kirlian imaging is that much of the work has been of a poor scientific standard and dogged by artefacts. His own findings have convinced him that all high-energy approaches to monitor subtle energy change are non-starters, as it is not possible to differentiate artefacts from real change in the structure under investigation.

Harry Oldfield however dismisses Kenyon's objections that the use of high frequencies must destroy any possibility of receiving the delicate wave emanations from tissues and cells, arguing that cellular resonance does not emanate from just one cell, but from the whole organism. This suggests that the Kirlian photographic image demonstrates the summation of human tissue and cellular resonance which is recorded on the photographic media.

The American researcher Nordenstromm wrote a book called *Closed Bio-Electric Circuits* in which he claims that electrical circuits play a far more important role in the body's attempts to maintain and heal itself than has been hitherto imagined. For example, the forces that attract white blood cells to a place where you may have a splinter are in fact electrical forces, because the inflammatory area where the splinter occurs develops a charge, the charge is opposite to that of the white blood cells. The search had been on for a long time to discover the chemical that was responsible, but Nordenstromm has shown that the responsible agent is not a chemical at all. He has also shown that the arteries and the veins act as conduits not only for blood but for electrical currents and can act over short or very long distances. The arteries, nerves, or any conductor of blood is a virtual electrical cable since the electromagnetic field is recorded and transmitted by the red blood cells.

The streamer effect comprises the following stages. A few electrons are first produced in the interelectrode space, are accelerated by the field and then ionize the air molecules, yielding an exponential growth in the number of electrons and positive ions. The electrons sweep quickly towards the anode (+ve) and the cluster of positive ions moves somewhat more slowly towards the cathode (–ve). When the positive ion cluster in the air gap reaches a critical density it strongly attracts the electrons, so that a large number of recombination events occur and photons of light are generated to such a degree that the cluster of positive ions becomes brightly luminous and travels at high speeds. Both positive and negative streamers move between the electrodes so that discrete balls of light move in various directions.

In air at high field strengths, the normal 'colour' of the stream is a bright blue, since the most frequent radiation is from highly excited nitrogen molecules. Ultraviolet radiation is also produced, and its intensity exceeds that of blue in most cases.

With all colour effects on photographic paper or film we should remember that electrons have no colour of their own. The excited particles penetrate to different depths depending on their speed. Colour film is made up of three layers of emulsion which during processing take on the three primary colours. As electrons lose their speed so rapidly in air, it is clear that the parts of the object close to the film are going to appear as coloured differently from the more distant parts. Even taking this into account there are still differences which cannot be explained by the closeness of the finger or object to the photographic medium. An example of this is the quoted work of Vittoria Marangoni with schizophrenic patients.

Assuming that non-physical energies exist, it is not rational to expect to measure them using instruments fashioned on detection methods of the five physical senses. By 'non-physical' we are referring to energies of a non-electromagnetic, non-sonic and non-gravitational variety; energies that do not directly stimulate our five senses and do not propagate in the four-dimensional space–time continuum, e.g. those which do not follow in inverse square law.

Although a large range of psychic and non-physical energy effects has been familiar for over a century, little advance in the level of theory has been observed. The significance of this failure is that no mere extension of the existing theoretical model of the natural world, even by the construction of a substantial new wing, is likely to accommodate psychical effects. It will be necessary to rebuild even the foundation. This necessity might have been foreseen from consideration of the unique manner by which we take cognizance of the psychic aspect of reality, as compared with the altogether different means by which we obtain our knowledge of its physical characteristics.

From a theoretical point of view, there are three methods of monitoring non-physical energies:

1.   A human being who has already developed other sensory systems and provides a read out (a medium).

2.   A living system, such as an animal, plant or human being, plus an attached electromagnetic or mechanical device to transduce these non-physical energies and give a coherent printout (Kirlian photography).

3.   A totally inanimate device based on a different system of logic which would both transduce and read out. This would be a development of the work of Harold Saxton Burr. So far as I know, machines do not exist in this category.

What is required is the development of a necessary and sufficient experimental protocol for obtaining consistent results no matter who does the experiment or where it is performed. The physiological parameters that can directly influence the nature and extent of the streamer discharge, and which can be altered by mental or emotional changes in the living organism need to be carefully monitored.

William Tiller, Professor of Materials Science at Stamford University, Conn. USA, identifies these as large changes in the electrostatic skin potential; changes in skin chemistry; changes in the dielectric properties of the skin; changes in the secondary electron emission characteristics from the skin and changes in the electrical impedance of the system.

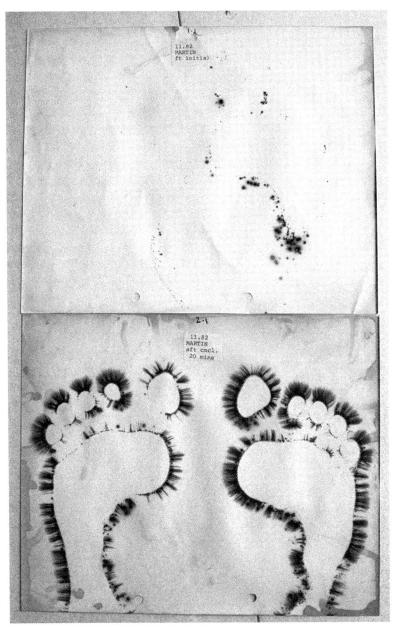

*Examples of Kirlian photographs of feet before (top) and after
(bottom) acupuncture treatment. Note the marked change in
configuration and extent of energy.*

~6~

Into the Unknown — the body electric

Kirlian Photography is an invaluable tool for investigating the 'shape' of the vital body compared with that of the physical vehicle. In my own case, it was the stimulus that led to the discovery of a more subtle, more sophisticated method which may lead us into new territory. As mentioned above, many of us have the ability to feel the emanation of standing waves particularly from human subjects, plants and stones. For some reason I have had the instinct to develop this facility in myself. You are invited to share my discovery and perhaps refine and develop it. I give it freely as it was given to me in that same spirit by my original mentor Andrew Glazewski and others.

It was with great interest that I came across an article in a specialist Russian magazine *AURA-Z* about the discovery of a 'hitherto unknown phenomenon' of the receptivity of human beings to emanations from cellular structures associated with a beehive. The author Viktor Grebennikov is a member of the Entomological Society of the Academy of Sciences which specializes in the study of bees and their nest making habits. He reports that

> *"whilst searching for something on my instrument-cluttered laboratory table, I accidentally passed my hand over a container full of debris from the old nests of the subterranean sweat bee. While my hand lingered over these long since lifeless fragments of living material, I felt... warmth and some kind of prickling or twitching in the fingers. I was loathe to trust my own senses, and once more passed my palm over the cells – again I notice the warmth and tremors of a sort in my fingertips and joints.*

> *By moistening and earthing the fragments, I ascertained*
> *that the cause of these phenomena was not electricity; a*
> *thermometer confirmed that 'warmth' was not the cause;*
> *an ultra-sonic frequency meter could find no trace of a*
> *signal."*

Colleagues who became involved also experienced warmth, burning, a puff of warm wind, pressure changes, movement on the hand, pressure and giddiness. Others even felt a sour taste in the mouth.

The beehive material was taken to various outdoor and indoor locations. The subjects were chosen from a wide cross-section of the population and included labourers, students, school children, agronomists and science workers. It was found that this mysterious radiation uninterruptedly penetrated through any barrier – be it cardboard, metal or brick wall – thus displaying the characteristics of magnetic, electric and gravitational fields.

Careful studies revealed areas of unpleasant sensations at various distances from the beehive material as if an invisible electric web was functioning at a distance from the physical material. His conclusion was that

> *"the waves which radiate from multi-cellular structures – living*
> *or inanimate – are capable of affecting living organisms by*
> *changing their physiological condition".*

The writer, in seeking an explanation for this, referred to the work of the French Scientist Louis de Broglie who, in 1924, made a discovery which earned him a Nobel Prize in 1929 – his advancement of the theory of the wave property of matter, which is that around any object there exists an imperceptible but real wave field. These waves can form and generate 'standing waves' of varying degrees of complexity. This was seen as revolutionary in its time and, even now, we have made few inroads into understanding its implications. It is comforting to find historical evidence for a phenomenon which I thought for years was peculiar to me!

The studies of Harold Saxton Burr and the volume *Design for Destiny* by Edward Russell, intrigued me, and it is worth at this point dwelling on the theory. All the constituents of living matter, whether functional or structural, are in a constant state of flux. Our lungs, brains, bones, skin, and principal muscles are completely regenerated in around 22 weeks. Some mysterious mechanism rebuilds dying molecules exactly as they were before, bearing in mind the incredible complexity of the body, the thousands of different chemicals, the liquids in constant circulation, all forming in the right time and in the right place.

Russell postulated that all living forms are controlled by electromagnetic fields. These are the organizing mechanisms that keep things in shape and build, maintain and repair them through constant changes of material. Therefore organs, cells, molecules and atoms are subordinate to these electromagnetic fields. Their existence can be measured in pure direct current potentials which vary not only within the living organism, but which radiate from it and are therefore readily measured by high-impedance voltmeters.

What particularly interested me was that not only physical conditions but mental conditions have their own associated field. Mentally unstable people display erratic voltage patterns before there are any obvious symptoms. I wondered what role the mind had, if any, in the production of fields. If our bodies need fields to survive the ever-changing cell structure, how much more must our minds need some mechanism for holding and using the knowledge that we have.

The existence of telepathy – namely the transmission of thought from one person to another – has been established conclusively by many researchers, including Dr. J. B. Rhine of Duke University. One of the many features of his and others' results demonstrates that the distance between the sender and receiver makes no difference. An experiment conducted one thousand miles apart was no more or no less effective than one conducted in adjacent rooms of the same building. Prof. Vasiliev, Professor of Physiology in the University of Leningrad, demonstrated the same, that thought acts at a distance and penetrates all obstacles. He established in a series of double-blind experiments that there was an energetic connecting link between two people situated a considerable distance apart; he showed that a suggestion or thought in one mind produced an effect across space in another mind – one of the classical demonstrations that thought has field properties. Neither concrete walls, lead chambers or Faraday cages made the slightest difference.

These fields, which Russell called T-fields (thought fields) also have the property of attaching themselves to any kind of matter of any shape or size. This is commonly evidenced by the blessing or cursing of objects, and by the effect on the atmosphere of a building where a terrible tragedy has taken place. The size of the object is immaterial – it can either be a wedding ring, or a six-storey building. These curious and unique timeless fields are independent of matter and can travel through space without attenuation.

It seemed to be that the body in general and indeed the brain itself was a collector and user of all these thoughts and memories which can exist apart from the brain. We have been used to – or should I say brainwashed into – thinking that the mind is a part of the body, hidden away in the recesses of the skull. I feel a more accurate hypothesis – possibly the 'hypothesis of best fit' as statisticians so neatly say – is to regard the body as a part of the mind, the solid bit in the middle.

When someone comes into a room and we feel uneasy about them, or indeed feel good about them, are we using our five senses or our mind? If the former, why do we sometimes feel uncomfortable about an immaculately dressed attractive person. This is surely the mind working as it is intended – to inform us, and protect us from danger. I would suggest that we detect the energy field – or aura – of other people 24 hours a day whether we are aware of it or not. Information about anybody is available to us – just by bringing them into mind. That's all we have to do. We have the inbuilt telepathic ability. This works both ways. We have all had the experience of suddenly feeling depressed for 'no reason'. Of course there is a reason! We just don't know what that reason is. If the feeling comes 'out of the blue' then it may well be that we are receiving negative impressions of a friend, contact or colleague. This may be a *crie de coeur*.

I have found that when this happens to me, I scan round or visualize all my friends and contacts. When I hit on the relevant person, the depression suddenly lifts, again for 'no reason'.

How can this whole function? In the *Journal of Parapsychology* 1962, No.3, we receive a further hint from a review by Milan Ryzl of a Russian volume, *Biologischeskaya Radiovyas*, by researcher B. B. Kazinsky.

> *"Kazinsky... developed an electromagnetic theory of telepathy which can be considered as one of the most elaborate theories*

> *of this kind. According to his conception, the nervous system of man during mental activity emits electromagnetic waves which, by means of the mechanism of electro-induction, give rise to corresponding processes in the nervous system of the percipient"*

It is doubtful if electromagnetic theory can itself fully explain this phenomenon which I am about to describe, but it probably forms the basis of it. It is my suspicion that electromagnetic fields are carriers or catalysts for more subtle fields of thought, that attach themselves like washing to a line.

Brainwaves themselves are so weak that they cannot be registered by instruments a few millimetres from the head. Telepathy works over vast distances which I suspect involves a repeating wave form but there is no more reason to believe that those tiny currents in the brain produce such effects directly than that we could shout across the Atlantic using the power of our voice. There may be two classes of effects and waves, one of which obeys the inverse square law (for example the heat from an electric fire) and the other consisting of quantum effects that do not.

The inverse square law postulates that if you double the distance between the transmitter and receiver, you don't just halve the power but quarter it. In mathematical terms the signal strength is inversely proportional to the square of the distance. It may be that the electric currents corresponding to mental activity are translated and transformed by some other radiation of a higher order than electromagnetism, which we could call biomagnetism. This latter may enjoy a greater degree of freedom and may comprise the missing link. We should not forget the ubiquitous magnetic field of the earth. Can electrical information be transmitted instantly along these magnetic fields? The more imaginative will realize that the circulating material in the body, blood, carries magnetically sensitive material in the form of iron. If we were to find that our thoughts can somehow influence the magnetic characteristics of the blood then... what happens if you move one magnetic field in another? Think on this. Regrettably we do not yet have the instruments of the sensitivity of the human body to record and measure such even sequences.

Assuming the reality of these radiations, my conclusion was that the main factor that prevents us using this so-called paranormal facility is that we do not believe in it and in consequence do not listen out for the signals. In the Russian experiments with the beehive material, the only difference between that situation and ours is that we do not focus on the amazing network of signals that assails us daily. In short, we ignore our feelings. How often have we heard people say self-depreciatingly, "Oh, it was just a feeling".

The process of incorporating this phenomenon into my work, which is that of sensitive and counsellor, was long, painful and drawn-out. It has taken me twenty years to refine a method that is objective and reliable.

Bearing in mind what we know of telepathy, and Burr's work and Russell's development of it, what was to prevent my 'talking' to these T-fields and 'asking' for a response? Supposing I activated my own nervous system to detect these fields – not all of them at once, but specific ones. If a humble computer can perform 16 different tasks at the same time, why should not the human brain/mind, an infinitely more sophisticated organ, be called to our service in this way?

If these fields are as ubiquitous as it seems, then it should be possible to use my mind to organize them. As we have found a correlation between acupuncture, Kirlian and palmistry, would it be possible to directly pick up the electrical equivalent of the Kirlian without the need to make a Kirlian picture?

A major application of the Kirlian photography method from the therapeutic view is its use as a diagnostic tool to assist people to restore the balance between their minds, bodies and spirits. In order to know how a client can be helped, it is necessary to get a feel of the situation. This can often happen immediately and instinctively when two or more people gather together in love and caring. Pragmatically this consists of a deliberate act of tuning in to or focusing on the patient. Some students will choose to spend a period of quietness; others will encourage the client to speak about what is on their mind. Very often, the presenting condition is peripheral to the actual cause of the distress.

Here is a vital practical exercise that can be performed by anyone either privately or at a seminar or course. For the sceptical it is a simple matter to experiment with the phenomenon yourself. The writer finds that 90% of participants in his courses and seminars can feel these radiations.

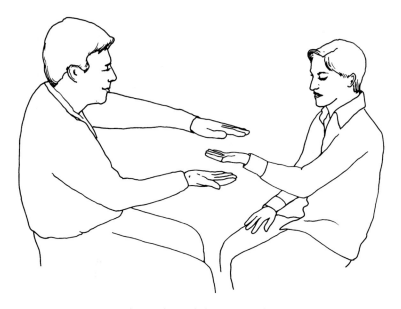

The reality of the energy field.
An experiment that anyone can perform.

Sit down with a friend. Get them to remove rings, watches, etc and place their left hand, palm upwards, in front of them, supported if necessary by a cushion. Place your right hand, palm upwards, beneath their hand; your left hand on top. Move your hands slowly towards the hand of your partner. It is important to suspend any judgemental activity and try to keep the mind blank. Simply 'listen' to your hands. Take notice of any tingles, warmth, images, body impressions, impulses. Do not ignore any symptoms, however apparently unrelated. Imagine that there is going to be an electrical dialogue – or silent talking – between your hands and the hand of the client.

Where is an impression occuring in the hand? At the end of the fingers? At the side? At the base? In the vast majority of cases, the client will start to feel after a few moments either a tingle or heat/cold in their hands. It is most important to make an immediate note of where the reaction occurs. The student may also feel a reaction but not necessarily in the same part of my hands. This tingle is a sign that communication is taking place between the energy fields or auras. It's like the interaction between two electrical maps.

However, there is a further stage. After the client reports what has happened the student should withdraw their hands, mentally clear the field, and repeat the action. Such a clearing can be done by flicking the hand as if removing water. The action should be repeated. The client will inevitably report a feeling in a different part to their hands. Repeat as often as necessary until the impressions die out or remain in the same part of the hand. It is common for up to six different passes to be necessary.

It is my submission (as yet unproven) that these bar codes contain information about the subject. As we have the ability to tune into them we also have the ability, the means, unbeknown to ourselves, to decode or realign. For this process to take place, conscious knowledge is not necessary. This process may comprise a part of the mysterious mechanism known as 'healing'.

The uniquely valuable aspect of this phenomenon is this: the location on the hand in which the impression is felt indicates the next step that the client must take in order to fulfil their own destiny. In some strange way the energy field 'knows' what the next step is. For example, if there is an impression in the middle finger, then the client needs to examine their job situation. If it is at the side of the finger, then there is a conflict in the job situation that needs to be resolved.

Not all sensations are covered in the chart. Heat or cold on the back of the hand indicates self-consciousness, the 'what will people think of me' situation. This is very common in those who are seeking to develop their healing or psychic ability. It will often be the first reaction which shows that if personal development is to take place, self-consciousness must be cast aside. A circle of heat in the centre of the palm is an indication of the ability to receive or give healing. We can define healing in this context as the ability to penetrate the energy field of other people. In some instances it indicates the need to receive healing. To check this, place the hands adjacent to the shoulders of the client, or over their head. Hold the hand still for a few moments. If heat is felt, continue the action until the heat dies down.

There are some people – albeit a very few – who are not affected by this exercise and to their consternation feel nothing. In the long experience of the writer, it has observed that these subjects are inevitably nursing some type of deep psychological trauma. In normal instances the energy field surrounds the body like a cloak. This may be the reason why such subjects complain of feeling cold when the outside temperature is warm. In these cases the aura has withdrawn

Name _____

Notes
1. SHARP PAINFUL LINE
2. STRONG 'PRICK'
3. WARM CIRCLE OF ENERGY
4. LINE DOWN TO BASE OF HAND
5. PRICKS AT FINGERTIPS
6. NO REACTION

Record of hand impressions as recorded on a chart. This shows the many and varied impressions that are perceived.

or become distorted and is not able to perform its silent function of acting as an unceasing transmitter/receiver between the subject and others. Counselling is particularly required in these cases.

The discovery which I modestly claim is one which has a significant implication for the future of diagnostic medicine. The changing patterns and the response to the exercise described above indicate areas of life which need attention **in the interests of the future.** Further, they are given in the **order** in which they must be achieved. Through some mechanism which we can only intuit, the energy field surrounding the living object is capable of reporting what has to be done if it is to work in symmetry and fulfil itself.

An essential assumption in my work is Jung's concept of the 'collective unconscious'. This involves the belief that all minds are in contact at some level.

For those of my readers who have maintained their credulity, it is further possible to 'project' the aura upon any convenient object of choice. This is the basis of psychometry. Objects such as rings are capable of holding information – in ways in which we can only conjecture at the moment – about the wearer. In addition, any chosen object can be used as a structure on which to project the identity of the chosen person or subject. In my case I used an onyx egg. The field of the person can then be 'interrogated', and measurements and evaluations can be made via 'interference patterns' generated by them. It is not necessary to know anything about the person, in fact it is a disadvantage to have any information about them in the conscious mind.

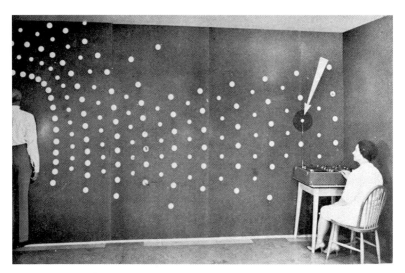

*Early measurements of standing waves coming
from an individual.*

There are many types of configuration coming from a living being, a composite between the functioning of the mind, the body and the spirit. Through mental clarity the student can address the one or the other. I call the configuration below the personal 'bar code' of the person which appears to contain information coded in the sub-sections.

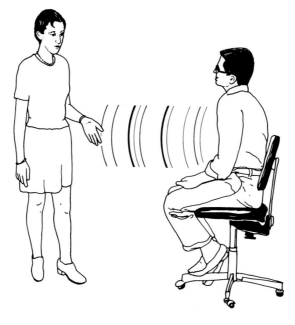

The hand being used to detect the radiations.

As work is done, it is often reported that clients feel more at ease with themselves, and it may be that the aura of a sensitive person acts like a sponge and 'mops up' some of the interference patterns in the client. The topic of healing – or making whole – is outside the scope of this book, but I suggest that healing is about the balancing of the subtle bodies and the temporary cancelling out of interference patterns. A study of parapsychological literature – barely touched on above – is that the property of the human energy field is its ability to affect other fields at a distance. Kirlian photography may well be monitoring this phenomenon. Such modulation could partly explain the mechanism of prayer.

There is another method of assessment which some may care to attempt. A high impedance (>100 Megohms on 300 MV DC) digital voltmeter is used. Electrodes connect the meter with the left and right hands via copper or brass rods. At the start of the treatment the standard voltage reading across the body is measured. It can range from 10 MV to about 60 MV. Using the machine partly as a bio-feedback tool, I ask the patient to relax whilst looking at the meter and they are asked to 'will' the meter to register 0 MV. The quicker the voltage tends to zero, the more able are they to relax. People with high stress levels maintain a high voltage. Levels of 50 or 60 MV are common with those who nurse guilt or anger.

A patient being measured at the start of a session.

After my treatment, which consists of a combination of counselling and healing, the client is tested again. If the treatment has succeeded, the voltages start at a lower level and diminish with more regularity and with greater speed. Sometimes the left is positive with respect to the right, followed by a change in polarity. This is found to be associated with the predominance of feeling over thinking, and vice versa – the comparative activity of the left and right brain. When the work has been unsuccessful, there is no change in the voltages.

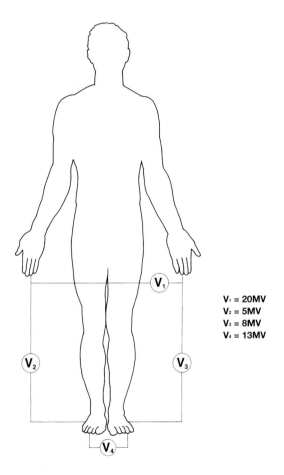

V₁ = 20MV
V₂ = 5MV
V₃ = 8MV
V₄ = 13MV

Voltage measurements from hand to hand, foot to foot. This diagram shows typical voltage grids. The more irregular the results, the more unstable is the subject.

A refinement to the method includes the measurement of the differences in voltage hand to hand, feet to feet, hand to feet on left and right.

Anyone can try these experiments for themselves. Suitable apparatus is a SMART 2 Digital Multimeter, available from such stores as Tandy. The output leads should be attached to copper rods, and the use of conducting gel will ensure good electrical contact.

Other analogous experiments with acupuncture treatment show that electric fields within the body change after the practitioner has worked.

I suggest that the aura of the practitioner as well as the techniques in use have an effect on the client, merely by virtue of focusing on him or her. We all know of people who have a calming effect on us by their very presence. The effect is silent, unspectacular and often not noticed during the time spent together.

I find this method very non-invasive since good therapy should not consist of telling people what to do. The contract should be between the client and their own higher self.

Incidentally, the word therapy comes from the Greek *theraps* – a companion or servant. We are there to assist, to prompt, to listen, to empathize, to share the pains and the joys, to help illuminate, to act as a catalyst.

For my work I design charts and diagrams and project the attributes of the person on to them. At certain points on the chart, I feel a small shock – or shocks – in my hand. I believe that I am picking up the very small standing wave patterns which can be created by the mind. This is a most useful discovery, which will bear a great deal of examination in years to come. It appears that it is possible for the human mind to by-pass the conscious mind of another mind and 'interrogate' the nature and extent of the problems, skills and abilities possessed by the subject. This is the basis for my work and is a more formal extension of the 'feelings' that, for example, a mother will have for her child, or a wife for her husband. In common parlance, a person 'just knows' when something is wrong. I have taken this mechanism and developed it. The functioning is best, incidentally, when I know nothing about the subject. This is because any information in my conscious mind can and does interfere with the reception of the data.

Every time I give a reading to the client, further changes occur in their field. For example when a correct solution is identified, the

waveforms on the charts change their configuration on further examination. There has been an interaction between my mind and the
mind of the client outside the constraints of time and space to discern
'in advance' the correct solution for the development of that person.
Time is an illusion, a mere reference point for the logical left brain. It
has no place in mysticism!

Bearing the above in mind, what is the function of the aura or
energy field? There is general agreement amongst sensitives that it has
a two-fold function; to give information and to protect us. Imagine a
group of people at a party. All their energy fields would be impinging
and interacting. Any anomalies in the individual energy field would
allow the formation of complex interference patterns, leading to con-
fusion of thought. The function of a regular energy field may be to
act as a barrier – or filter – against unwanted and disharmonious
fields from others. Energy cannot be passive – two way 'traffic' of
information is implicit.

Our energy field is our unique imprint on the universe. Only
when viewed from the constrictions of our five senses is it limited or
finite. It may be found in the future that mantras, prayers, medita-
tions are a way of preserving the integrity of the energy field and thus
form a living vibrant barrier between us and the cocktail of electromagnetic fields which, whilst they perform a vital role in telecommu-
nications technology, may also be the cause of so much mental and
physical disturbance in this civilized world.

~7~

Future directions — the Nature of Reality

The development of modern science presents us with major challenges to grasp the complexity and dimensions of the modern world. Take the atom. We all know that atoms are the building blocks of matter. But do we really appreciate how small they are? If the characters in this book were reduced to the size of an atom, not only would they fit in a grain of sand, but there would be enough space remaining for all the texts in the 24 million books in the world. There are the same number of inter-neural connections in our brain as there are leaves on the ten billion trees in the Amazon basin. Does this not strain the human imagination? Can we really understand this? I am reminded of a part of the Book of Common Prayer, 'the peace of God which passes all understanding'. In other words, 'Don't try to understand it with your finite mind.'

To address the subject of Kirlian photography, indeed any subject which might traverse more than one dimension, we need what is called a 'scientific (or creative) imagination', not the act of committing intellectual suicide.

For example the distinction between mind and body is an artificial dichotomy, a discrimination based far more on the peculiarity and intransigence of intellectual understanding than on the actual nature of life. To differentiate between one and the other is like trying to decide at which point one end of a stick becomes the other. Plato recognised the limitations of measuring the non-physical world using scientific instruments, themselves objects belonging to the physical world. Plato relegated the 'real' world to the status of shadows cast by its real elements. In other words, electrons, photons and other entities entering into our model of the world are in the nature of hypothesis, acceptable on a provisional basis only and liable to be superseded as our vantage point shifts and develops. Gross matter such as composes a table or a chair stands in no fundamental relation to reality, being only elements belonging to the more primate theoretic models we construct for ourselves in the 'nursery' from the raw materials of experience.

What tools, therefore, do we adopt for our initial stance in our search for anything? If we take the mind as a starting point, we work our way from the relatively unknown to the known; while in the opposite case we have the advantage of starting from something known, that is from information given by the five senses. The world of energy is still more obscure to us than the visible body; our knowledge of these energies can only be gleaned indirectly, and the methods to evaluate them are often mediated by conscious functions which have many inbuilt weaknesses and propensities to deceive.

Almost by definition, discoveries are ahead of their time and must often wait until the awareness of the larger community attaches significance to the implications.

Matter is real, but reality is more than matter. Albert Einstein stated that there is no such thing as matter, which is merely an illusion created by the vibrational speed of various forms of energy. Are there more of the basic elements of creation in the psychic world or the physical world? What if the psychic world is the primary and the physical world is the derived world, and not vice versa as the majority of scientists still believe. We are not able in some behaviourist moment to reject primary elements in favour of secondary elements whose existence is conditional on the former. The present tactics of ignoring the primary on the grounds of uncertainty in favour of the secondary is temporary expediency. Ultimately we shall have to grapple with the primary, or disciplines such as psychology will remain isolated from the most characteristic feature of its object of study, viz: the psyche. Can we build primary experiential components into the model of the cosmos, even risk having a revolutionary impact on all extant theories by relegating time and space firmly to the category of secondary elements?

Concerning the above reference to chairs and tables, we perceive such objects without relatively slowly moving energies, merely as other things vibrating at the same rate. Hence all objects that vibrate within the physical range appear as solid, but this is of course to a large extent illusory. If, for example, all the space between the atoms in a human body were to be removed, then the solid bit would be less than the size of a grain of sand. This scientific fact should revolutionize the way we see people.

As C. S. Lewis remarked, "Don't confuse the bundle of atoms standing in front of you for a human being." As there are an infinite number of different vibrationary rates, so there are an infinite number of universes.

Reality includes consciousness which is not measurable directly. Studies of the aura in general, and Kirlian in particular, contain pointers to the place of holistic diagnosis in mental and physical health. How do we see things? In Kirlian photography we have the opportunity to see information about diseases in the pre-formative state. Radionics perform a similar task, picking up disturbances before the symptoms become apparent.

However, if Kirlian is to stand on an authoritative platform along with more established methods, a scientific basis needs to be established. The association of Kirlian with mystics and unorthodox healers undoubtedly vitiates its receptions by the scientific and medical community as a whole. It is to the benefit of all researchers to examine the scientific method and transfer it to their own discipline. It is necessary for Kirlian researchers to speak the same language and use the same terminology as the scientific community in order to become accepted.

Also, any challenge to commercial interests, such as drug companies, by offering the possibility of quick and accurate testing will inevitably lead to a form of protectionism, as most of the key researchers in the USA have found to their cost.

Kirlian may well strengthen its case by aligning itself with longer established accepted methods such as traditional Chinese medicine, e.g. acupuncture, plus homoeopathy, chiropractic, etc.

Doctors may acknowledge that at all levels of medicine measurement techniques are sometimes crude and interpretation somewhat limited. 'Western Medicine', far from being the coherent system we would like to imagine, is characterised by enormous variations in diagnosis and treatment. One nation's chosen treatment may be considered malpractice by another, and the recommended dosage of a drug in one country may be ten or twenty times higher than in another. An example is the attitude to marijuana. Not all doctors within a given country diagnose and treat identically, and they are influenced by the culture, medical training, social pressures and the expectations of the patients. These variations also apply to Kirlian Photography diagnosis.

The real difference is that Western medicine expects a biochemical approach to diagnosis, whereas Eastern cultures mostly entertain an 'energy' diagnosis, such as estimations of the 'yin' and 'yang' potentials as in Chinese medicines. Kirlian can be seen as an attempt to look at Eastern methods of diagnosis with Western eyes.

Although Western medicine may have its deficiencies, no single alternative diagnostic method has been sufficiently successful and convincing for all practitioners to be convinced of starting again with a new set of assumptions. This is unlikely with Kirlian, since the number of variables is so great as to make a definitive statistical survey hugely expensive.

An accumulation of anecdotal evidence – which is the most that the typical Kirlian practitioner is able to produce – will slowly close the gap between the scientific and unscientific, supported and unsupported data.

However, some differences in approach do not arise from intellectual inferiority but from quality and extent. Non-orthodox procedures are by nature individualized, and since such practitioners tend to rely on their intuition more often than with the case of an orthodox practitioner, the scope for dialogue is limited by this. For research purposes, the main benefit of Kirlian could be to indicate to the scientific community wider remits for research routes. At present the stumbling point for many scientific thinkers is the difficulty quantifying the information in the streamers and inner corona which comprise the aura, though sterling efforts are being made by many Kirlian researchers to quantify and computer analyse the pictures. Meanwhile, a positivistic approach prevails in conventional thinking. A discipline is only accepted if its tenets are recognised as familiar.

Truth – or a reliable working hypothesis – is arrived at by two methods of studying phenomena; reductionistic (splitting things down to the basic elements and trying to work out how they behave) and holistic (an overview of the whole organism and its relationship to the universe). The two methods can be complementary. Holistic thinking can and should include analysis; reductionistic thinking should include imaginative and lateral thinking.

Holistic enthusiasts should not claim that Eastern philosophy is superior to Western thinking. From a given set of observations and data, many different laws can be educed. We can never be sure that we have the correct set.

Einstein, in a letter to M. Solovine dated 7 May 1952, wrote about "the almost problematic connection between the world of ideas and that which can be experienced". He stressed that there is "no logical path" between theoretical concepts and our scientific observations. One is brought into concordance with the other by an "extra-logical (intuitive) procedure".

The divide between Kirlian and other disciplines may never be bridged using rational argument; rather, the sheer weight of evidence will convince those antagonists of the necessity of doing further research.

The interaction between mind, body and spirit – free energy – is not directly accessible to observation and measurement. It is the dissipation of energy around the human body which is recorded by an increasing number of methods including direct observation, invasive and non-invasive methods. Kirlian energy photography is capable of giving us valuable clues about the shift of man's vital energies and should be correlated with the results of other disciplines, old and new, to further our understanding of mankind's true deep nature.

What is the current situation of acceptability of subjects such as Kirlian? Much hard work has been done by thousands of researchers. Over 600 scientific papers and articles have been published. However, so formidable are the number of subjects that Kirlian touches on, that definitive statements cannot be made. We do not even understand the nature of electricity, let alone the nature of the ability of a magnetic field to influence the bio-energetic field of another person.

At the International Conference on Kirlian Photography in 1990, Bernard Grad discussed the difficulties of obtaining research funding. Dr. Grad is well able to view this matter with historical perspective, since from 1949 to 1985 he was research assistant lecturer and later assistant professor at the Allan Memorial Institute of Psychiatry at the McGill University in Montreal. He has had over 100 articles published and is a member of the American Association of Cancer Research. He describes himself as a scientist and a biologist who has an interest in healing. He observed that *"the majority of research is conducted outside a university setting although inside the universities is where the money is. In general, these institutions do not want to link themselves not only with Kirlian, but with such topics as healing, parapsychology. This is due to the vast difference in their mental set. Many university researchers, particularly in the USA, have put their career on the line by proclaiming an interest in such matters as Kirlian."*

At the same conference the Chairman, Michael Endecott, of the British Institute of Complementary Medicine, remarked thus:

"Funding organizations are almost invariably reticent about looking at any venture which does not fall into their established paradigms. These paradigms are things which are scientifically acceptable. Way back in 1966, acupuncture was introduced into this country for the first time on TV, and the whole of the medical establishment in the UK said that it was nonsense. It can't work because there is no neurological pathway and therefore it is not viable. Today the UK sees over 600 medical doctors in the NHS using a limited form of acupuncture to promote pain control.

We can only move forward by bringing the complementary therapies into a line where the research parameters are acceptable to scientific evaluation. It does not mean today that the essential humanity and compassion which is the essential part of complementary medicine has to be lost. If you are not careful, when you put it into the laboratory it is that essential atmosphere which becomes hardened, and therefore the results are that much more difficult to quantify.

We should be under no illusions – we do have a problem. But, there is a demand in the NHS for fully qualified complementary practitioners who are capable of working alongside medical colleagues. We are using the word alternative selectively since it sometimes leads to misunderstanding. Everyone is working for the good of the patient and that will eventually succeed. The process of opening the minds of the public is a slow but essential process. However, there are positive signs. In 1990, three UK polls; Mori, Mintel, BBC radio found that 80% of the public wanted 'alternative medicine' on the NHS. The British Council of Complementary Medicine, a national charity, was incorporated in September 1994 as an umbrella body to further interest in these fields."

The typical attitude of the scientist will probably be: "Until I can get a handle on it, I remain sceptical." My reply is two-fold. First, a quote from C. G. Jung. "We should not fall into the fashionable error of saying that because we cannot prove anything we should call it a fraud." Second, I simply say: "If it works, use it!" I rest my case.

Bibliography

Adamenko, V. G., Kirlian, S. D. Sov. Pat. No. 209968, 1966

Adamenko, V. G., Inushin, V. M., Kirlian, S. D. and V. Kh. *Problems of Bioenergetics.*, Alma Ata: Kazakh State Univ., 1969

Babbitt, E. *The Principles of Light and Colour*, New York, University Books Inc. 1967

Bagnall, O. *The Origin and Properties of the Human Aura*, Samuel Weiser Inc. 1975

Karagulla, S. *Breakthrough to Creativity*, Santa Monica, De Vorss and Co. 1967

Marangoni, V., Evangelopoulou, T. and Yfantopoulus, J. 'Kirlian Photography: A tool in the diagnosis of psychopathology', *J. Biol. Photog.* Vol. 56, No. 3, 1988

Ostrander, and Schroeder, L. *Psychic Discoveries Behind the Iron Curtain*, Abacus, Sphere Books, 1973

Reichenbach, Baron Karl von *The Odic Force: Letters on a Newly Discovered Power in Nature*, Boston, 1854

Reichenbach, K. von *The Odic Force*, New York, University Books, 1968

Saxton Burr, H. and Northrop, F. *The Electro-dynamic Theory of Life*, New York, 1962

Saxton Burr, H., *Blueprint for Immortality*, The C. W. Daniel Company, London, 1972

Tansley, D. *The Raiment of Light*, London, Routledge & Kegan Paul,

Zimmerman, J. T. 'Electromagnetic Correlates of Laying-on-of-Hands (Therapeutic Touch)', *Newsletter of the Bio-Electro-Magnetics Institute*, 1: No. 1, page 3, 1989

Index